JOURNEY

ALAN WANZENBERG

JOURNEY

The Life and Times of an American Architect

PRINCIPAL PHOTOGRAPHY BY WILLIAM ABRANOWICZ

Editorial Director: Suzanne Slesin
Production: Dominick J. Santise, Jr.
Photography and Archival Research: Michelle Rose
Assistant Editor: Deanna Kawitzky
Text Consultant: Ian Phillips

POINTED LEAF PRESS, LLC.
WWW.POINTEDLEAFPRESS.COM

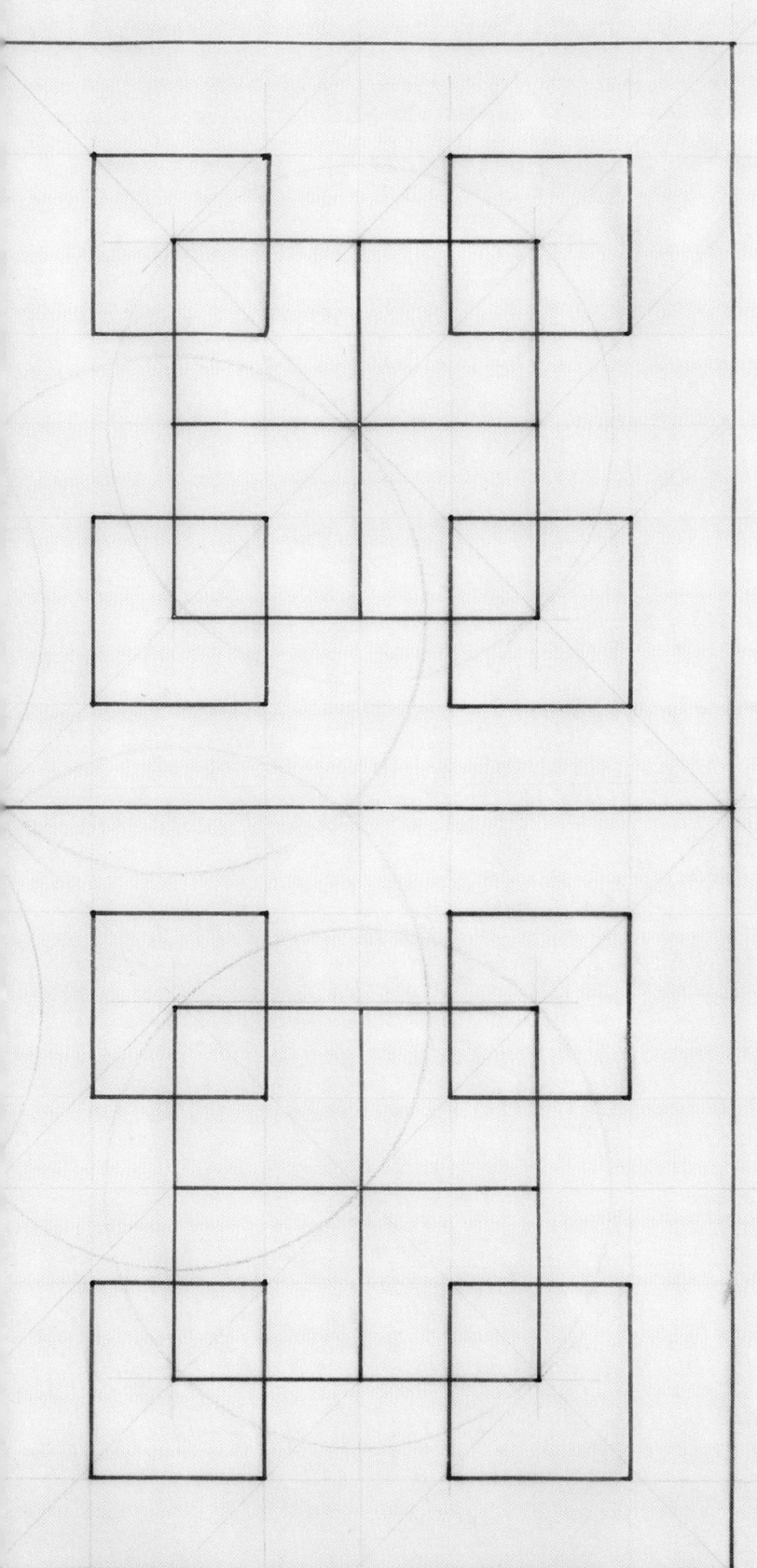

CONTENTS

ON THE ROAD TOGETHER 6

1
STARTING OUT 8

2
DESTINATIONS:
TEN PROJECTS 36

3
COMING HOME 222

INDEX 238

ACKNOWLEDGMENTS 240

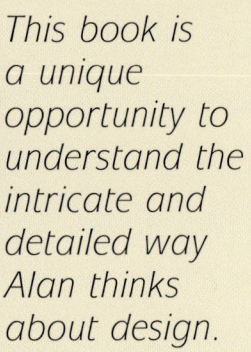

This book is a unique opportunity to understand the intricate and detailed way Alan thinks about design.

1. Beth's bathroom at 10 Gracie Square, done in Pewabic Studios tile, was finished in the mid-1980s.

2. Alan, left, Beth, and Jed in Kyoto, Japan, in 1993.

3. The archway between the entrance gallery and the living room in Beth's apartment was designed by Alan.

4. Alan and Beth in Bali, Indonesia, on New Year's Day of 1994.

5. Beth and Alan in New York in the early 1990s.

6. Jed found the Gothic white marble mantelpiece that is the centerpiece of the library.

ON THE ROAD TOGETHER

In 1980, over the Labor Day weekend, I was staying in the Hamptons with my old friend Tommy Dean and the producer Lester Persky. With my then-husband James DeWoody, we were all invited to a party on Lily Pond Lane in East Hampton given by Thomas Ammann, the handsome up-and-coming art dealer from Zürich. The Warhol crowd was in attendance, as most were staying at the house. Young, attractive, and extremely animated, I remember meeting the glamorous Barbara Allen, the writer Bob Colacello, and others including Averil Meyer, Bianca Jagger, Fred Hughes (Andy's business manager), and the adorable (and robust, by all accounts, that weekend) John Samuels, Jr. Jed Johnson was there with Alan Wanzenberg, and it was clear when I met them that a deep but private attachment had developed between them, despite the fact that Jed had been living with Andy for over a decade and Alan was similarly involved.

In 1988, I bought an apartment at 10 Gracie Square that John Fairchild, the publisher of *Women's Wear Daily*, had previously owned. The rooms were well-proportioned and the setting was special, as the apartment overlooked the East River. The apartment was in need of serious work, so I hired Jed and Alan at the recommendation of old friends who had recently completed a project with them. Conventionally speaking, Alan did the architecture and Jed did the decoration. But, as I quickly learned, their personal relationship produced an intense involvement that added a thoughtful and important cohesiveness to the design process. Alan quickly went to work, adding details where previously there had been none, thus creating enhancements to the architecture that both respected and enriched the original. The largest undertaking was the design of my master bathroom. I'd recently visited the restored Pewabic Studios in Detroit. Working with the original glaze formulas from the Pewabic heyday of production during the Arts & Crafts Movement at the beginning of the twentieth century (and now producing tile), I was intrigued with the possibility of using this material. Fortunately, given their deep affinities for this movement, Alan and Jed embraced the idea immediately and came up with the iconic, complex, beautiful design that I still live with today, as well as with other later elements, such as the great Gothic cabinet we found in London and the marble and tile mantelpiece in the library, an early example from the English Arts & Crafts era. Although I had knowledge of the Arts & Crafts Movement, working with Alan and Jed opened my eyes to it in a much deeper way. On our travels to historic homes, and during shopping excursions, I received a hands-on design education. I used to walk through Jed and Alan's apartment and just look at their library and furniture, always incredibly impressed with their eye and talent. Jed seemed to have this innate sense of what looked good, and Alan had a much more scholarly knowledge of the various movements.

In over 30 years of living in my apartment, and even though the decor has changed, I have never altered any of the architectural elements that Alan designed. I always felt that these details were what should have been there initially when it was built in 1929. Obviously, by the end of the process, we had become great friends. Alan loves to organize trips, and Jed and I were always happy to come along. We traveled to many architectural sites, not only in America but also in England, where we visited Standen, Red House, Wrightwick Manor, and other great English Arts & Crafts houses. We drove around hilariously in an oversized Daimler, ordered by the concierge of the hotel when Alan asked him to hire a car for us. When it arrived, Alan was reluctant to ask what it cost lest he come off as a hick from America. Later, we ventured to Japan (the sublime rock gardens of Kyoto), Java (the mysterious monument Borobudur), and Thailand (arriving by chance at the Jim Thompson House, where we were so taken by his collections that we took the tour twice!).

And I'm happy to say that these trips continue to occur. Recently, I visited Alan in Cape Neddick, Maine, where he shares a home with landscape architect Peter Kelly, his boyfriend of the past decade. Alan organized a wonderful trip to Prouts Neck, where we visited the Winslow Homer Studio. Then on to Skowhegan, where Alan is an active trustee, to walk the historic campus and visit the participants' studios. And on Saturday night, to a raucous party in Dark Harbor that went on until all hours. By no small coincidence, the event was the 40th anniversary of the release of the Rolling Stones' *Exile on Main Street*. The next morning, we went to Lincolnville to visit the painter Alex Katz and his wife, Ida, returning through the coastal towns and visiting the various museums in Rockland and Portland, as well as numerous art dealers. So you can well understand my pleasure and familiarity in writing this. Given the resonance of the title for me, no doubt this book will be a unique opportunity for the public at large to understand the intricate and detailed way Alan thinks about design and the context of the larger world around him.

Enjoy the journey!—Beth Rudin DeWoody

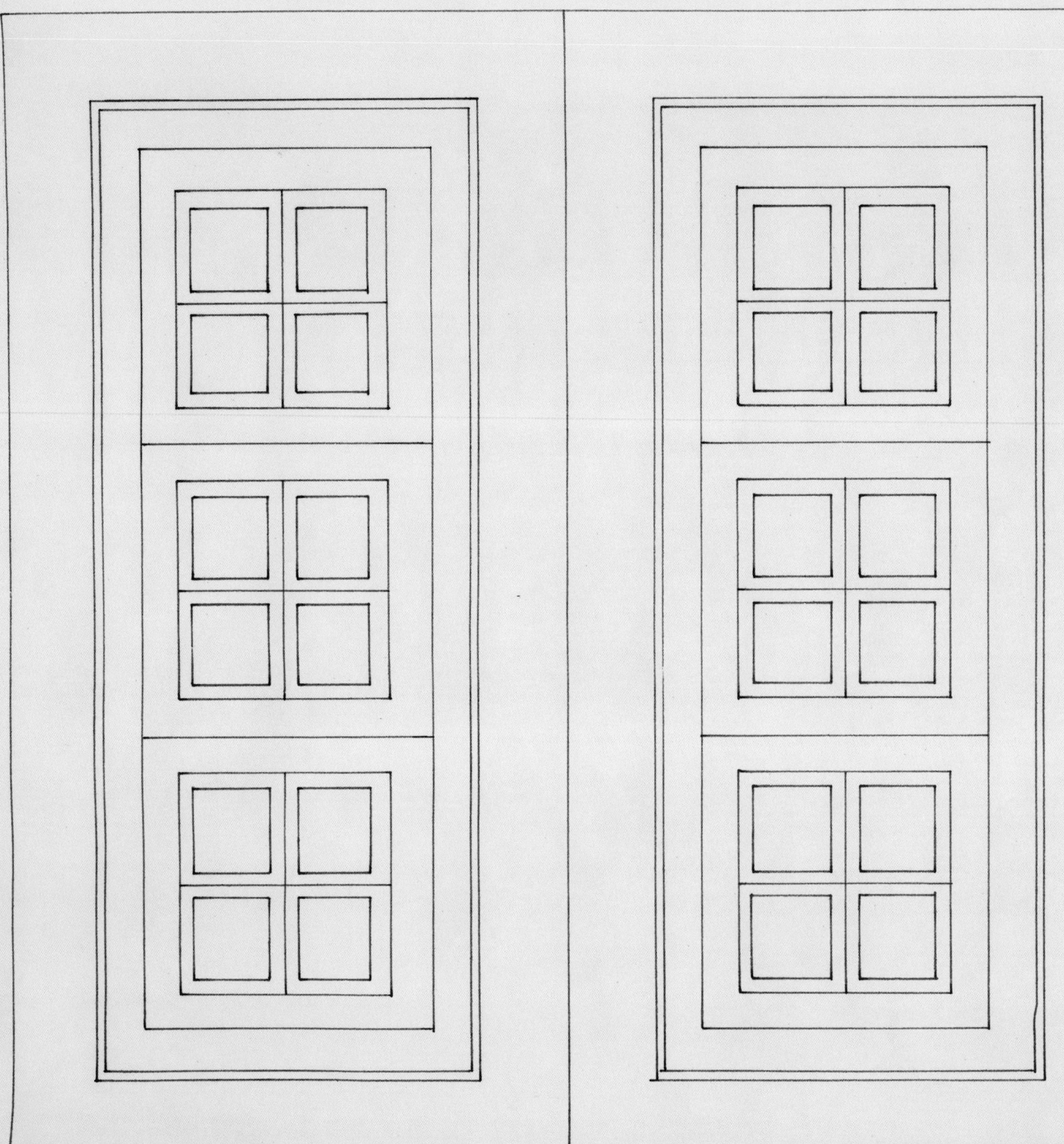

STARTING OUT

...from a physical place where recalling aspects of reality and illusion are combined in a manner of only relative importance.

Alan, left, with his grandmother and family in Evanston, 1955.

Classic Evanston architecture.

Contemporary home in Evanston.

Tennessee entrance hall, a Thorne Miniature Room.

As a child, I walked everywhere. In the fifties, kids walked everywhere. From kindergarten to the sixth grade, I'd walk to my elementary school and home for lunch and back for the afternoon class and then home when done. The route was most always the same, though it could vary. Sometimes, I'd take a shortcut. Sometimes, I would take the long way, but over time the rhythm and routine of my walking was very consistent. Occasionally I walked with a friend, but usually these walks were taken alone. Being alone, I would look at the houses in my neighborhood.

Most of the homes in my neighborhood of Evanston, Illinois, were built in the teens and 1920s. They were well-built, and I could intuit which were of a higher quality than others. I was curious and always engaged. They were comfortable but with tremendous stylistic and economic variations. As it was the 1950s, there were also newly built areas, such as those in small subdivisions that often consisted of only three or four houses. But these were the exception to the older fabric of the neighborhood. Fascinated by the older homes, I would study their half-timbered second floors or their Colonial Revival detailing. Occasionally there would be a gem of a house built under the influence of the Prairie School, or an architect's house that would stand out in a novel, self-conscious way from the other houses by seeming more informed and different in ways I would later identify as specific to my profession. I was never bored, even though the routine itself was often boring; but all the while, I could use my imagination. I am convinced that this simple act of walking every day, multiple times a day, stimulated my imagination in a profound way. I didn't evaluate what I saw. I just looked. I looked and was totally absorbed with what I saw.

Several times a year, for a number of years, I went to the Art Institute of Chicago with a neighbor whose name was Mary Robertson. Highly educated, capable, and probably frustrated with her domestic life, as many women like her were in the 1950s, she was an old-fashioned intellectual. She studied things in great depth and detail. Brusque and very blunt, she did not suffer fools easily. And although she had a grown-up daughter who was out of the house, Mrs. Robertson didn't seem like a woman who would naturally gravitate to a solitary kid like me.

Our excursions in the Art Institute would consist of slow and lengthy observations. She would make me stand in front of a painting or a work of art, and look at it with intense and focused absorption, which was an important early discipline for my visual acuity. One area of the museum we always visited was the Thorne Miniature Rooms, which was exactly as described: a group of 68 dioramas comprised of historic interiors in miniature (on a scale of one inch to one foot). Gifted to the museum in 1954 by Mrs. James Ward Thorne, the rooms were constructed between 1932 and 1940 by master craftsmen according to her specifications. Obsessive and beautifully made, they are a visual treasure of architectural history consisting of residential interiors from the late thirteenth century to the 1930s. Styles ranged from German Biedermeier to French Art Deco, to American Shaker and Japanese Traditional—an astounding array of history in a relatively small space. Mrs. Robertson would have me stand in front of a Thorne room for what seemed like hours on end. I would look at the room, absorb the details, and then articulate to her what I saw, albeit crudely at times. Though

Card games as pastimes.

Pinewood dirby model car.

YMCA logo.

Alan, right, with his mother and brother, Philip, on Lake Michigan.

sometimes tedious, these exercises proved invaluable to the development of my observational skills, my aesthetic language, and my awareness of style.

Boredom often accompanies childhood. Today, parents would recoil at the idea of their kids being bored, but my boredom fostered creativity and ingenuity. We made things like race cars for the Pinewood Derby or collected First Day Covers. Or I would learn Bolivia, the three-deck variation of the card game Canasta, with my grandmother and her friends. Boredom has its benefits. For me, since I could understand and articulate its benefits, I've needed what boredom provides—long periods of unstructured time. As a child and as an adult, these time blocks have served the purpose of cultivating my imagination.

THE YMCA

I grew up with two older brothers. To me, both were confident, successful, and good looking. My tendency to isolate myself may have come from being intimidated by them. My parents, in their way, understood this and got me involved with the local YMCA where my brothers had been members and, in particular, campers. At the time, the Y's motto was "mind, spirit, body," which was exemplified in its triangular-shaped logo. Throughout my life, I've found this motto an enduring way of quickly evaluating myself and my activities, as well as a method for maintaining balance.

The Y's program featured swim teams and clubs loosely organized by the neighborhood in which one lived. The Y also had a summer camp, Camp Echo, where I was sent for most of the summer, regardless of whether I wanted to go. The Y's mostly group-based activities demanded participation. Reluctantly, I began to socialize. I attended camp up to the age of 13. One year lapsed, and at 15 my dad sent me back to camp to work on the maintenance crew. When I was 16, I went back to work with the camp's kitchen crew—both jobs, in which I served dozens of campers, made me recall that, a few years earlier, I had been one myself. The irony wasn't lost on me, needless to say. The great benefit from that time was the work ethic that was instilled in me. Continuing in that way, again at the direction of my father, who was a civil engineer and mechanical contractor, I joined the plumbers union at the age of 17, and when I was 18, the pipefitters, working as an apprentice for two summers. I have worked continuously since.

CASTLE PARK, LAKE MICHIGAN

Perhaps the most important influence on my early design sensibility were the cottages at Castle Park. In the summers, my maternal grandmother decamped to Michigan, renting quarters at a resort called Castle Park comprised of numerous summer cottages inhabited by families from Grand Rapids and Chicago. The property had originated in the late 1800s as the estate of Chicago real-estate developer Michael Schwarz, who ultimately abandoned it. Schwarz, a bit of a grandiose figure, created a centerpiece that was a turreted castle—a real castle. After being abandoned, the property was reinvented as a boy's school until the Carter Brown and Parr families—both of Chicago and Tryon, North Carolina—bought Castle Park and made it a multi-generational summer resort. I always relished this aspect of Castle Park's demographics, which evoked a sense of continuity among the residents. And for four generations, my family summered there.

ALAN AS A PIPEFITTER, SUMMER OF 1968.

The Castle at Castle Park on Lake Michigan.

The fireplace in the Old Timers' Room at Castle Park.

The Meeting House at Castle Park.

Castle Park is located on Lake Michigan, between the industrial towns of Holland and Zeeland, the latter home to Herman Miller, one of the first American companies to produce modern furniture. To the north and south, respectively, were the raucous lakeside towns of Douglas and Saugatuck, Michigan, where the summer art colony of Ox-Bow was situated. Both locales are known for their impressive art galleries featuring both local and national works.

I have profound memories of Castle Park's unique architecture created by the virtuosic but humble Brown, who was a Renaissance man in his time. Brown built a series of charming cottages, all in a variety of small sizes with unique floor plans, often capable of being discretely shared by several families such as mine. Rustic and curious, with names such as Sandpiper, Barnswallow, Plantation House, Bandbox, and Ebenezer's Barn, they evoked the imaginative, simple life one could lead in the summer months, during which time evaporated. The cottages had appropriately minimal concern for bedrooms and baths, since most residents spent all day outdoors. What I also always remember was that each structure featured an element where families frequently socialized—either around a fireplace, a porch, or a veranda. Devoid of air conditioning like most summer cottages of that era, the dwellings included a sleeping porch and a small patio that allowed families to partake in the cooler outdoor air as much as possible. The small kitchen was really nothing more than a gesture as guests took most meals in the dining room at the Castle or lunched on the dunes.

The interior living spaces were large but cozy, with low ceilings that made them even more intimate by virtue of the darker woods of the walls and the often simple but luxuriously made upholstery that included beautiful window seats and sofas. The chairs in the cottages were all from Old Hickory Furniture, an American company, that since 1890 has produced handcrafted furniture in Indiana. The ladderback chairs with rush seats were simple Americana—a sensibility seen later in my work at Twin Farms in Vermont.

The quarters of the cottages I thought most evocative were those for sleeping. As a small boy, I either slept outdoors on a sleeping porch or indoors in the equivalent of a bunk bed built into the wall along a hallway that had large windows for air circulation. The width of the hallway was ample, allowing for guests to traipse back and forth. Years later, I would create something similar at my homes on Water Island.

In constructing the cottages, Brown recycled old materials including timbers, using new ones only where he had to. His cottages were intimate, functional, and enchanting. Castle Park as a whole was also sophisticated in the sense that someone had really thought about how to live in these environments. It also gave me my first notion of visual memory—a process in which I subconsciously absorbed many details and elements of architecture and design that I'd later recall in my own homes or my own work, or whenever I enter a similar dwelling. Often, what we remember, we recreate. Castle Park influenced everything in my life's early aesthetics. The place was a laboratory of learning for me, with each cottage being unique in its materials and its varied and interesting layout. Aside from its physical attributes, Castle Park afforded something else that I have long sought out and made a priority—time that's my own. Aside from the mornings, during which all the kids were in "play class," children were let out after lunch, a practice that afforded tremendous periods of unstructured time.

Certainly the time allowed for opportunities to take tennis lessons and ride horses, but for me, I had the time to walk on the dunes and explore with no supervision, no regimen. This unstructured block of time in the day was so important to my early creative and intellectual development. To do nothing for a child like me was to really do something with my own time, with my own interior world during this part of my life. Few other times during the year demanded so little of me.

MY PARENTS, HENRY AND DORIS

Duality had an important place in my early life, the prime example being my father's immigration from Germany as a young boy in the 1920s. Having arrived on Ellis Island and being quarantined there for several months, he never denied his early poverty and childhood, but never spoke much of it, either. Quickly assimilating and losing his accent, he cherished the opportunities America gave him. My mother, on the other hand, came from a distinguished background that could be traced back to the eighteenth century, likely making her eligible for the Daughters of the American Revolution. Given the business achievements of her relatives in the early twentieth century, she was established and confident. My parents had a very solid marriage. For several reasons, some of which I understood, and some of which I didn't, they always lived below their means, which wasn't unusual for the times. Today, such living is nearly unheard of. The values they stressed were modesty, independence, and humor, explicit to the notion to not take oneself too seriously. I grew up in a secure, comfortable environment, but one where you were expected to work, which I did at an early age.

So, from this environment of a loving, earnest dad and an equally loving but astringent and critical mother, along with competitive older brothers and a competitive school, layered with nascent sexual realizations, came my desire for independence.

OUTWARD BOUND

Another experience from this period that deserves mention is attending Outward Bound, a not-for-profit organization then new to America that develops personal growth and social skills by partaking in challenges in the outdoors. It was the volatile summer of 1968, especially in Chicago, where the Democratic Convention was to be held. I had worked in the pipefitters union that summer, but Outward Bound was something I wanted to experience. I had researched the program and sought it out. My parents were approving but not involved.

I went to Outward Bound for a month prior to starting my senior year in high school, and the experience was profound. Outward Bound, with its motto, "To serve, to strive, and not to yield," developed confidence and self-awareness through specific physical challenges. The experiences gave me a maturity that I had not had before. The particular Outward Bound location I sought was Hurricane Island, in Penobscot Bay, off the coast of Maine. The course, starting in mid-August, lasted less than a month. Attended only by guys, the daily routine was vigorous: We were up before sunrise for a day filled with various sailing and climbing exercises, utilizing the surrounding waters and the abandoned rock quarry on the island. The many activities allowed little time for reflection, as most were group oriented except for the "solo," where one was left alone on one of the numerous nearby small uninhabited islands for four days and three

Classic armchair, from Old Hickory Furniture.

Doris and Henry Wanzenberg on their wedding day, October 12, 1941.

Outward Bound logo.

The original buildings at Hurricane Island, Maine.

Alan and his mother at the Coconut Grove in Los Angeles, 1961.

The Palace Hotel in San Francisco.

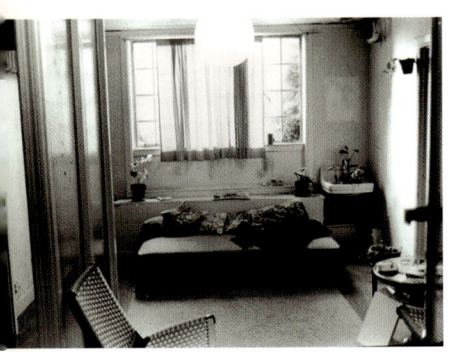

Alan's apartment on College Avenue, in Berkeley, early 1970s.

Angela Davis, Los Angeles, 1969.

nights. Expected to forage for food (after lessons provided by how-to handbooks such as Euell Gibbons' *Stalking the Blue-Eyed Scallop),* one was sent out with only a tarp, a sleeping bag, a few matches, and fresh water. Gibbons was somewhat of a revolutionary, a gifted nature and food writer who celebrated the joys of foraging in the wild. Left alone like this and certainly cut off and unaware of the riots and civil disobedience happening in Chicago to which I would have been drawn, I reflected on simple things like the weather, the water, and nature, and ate very little. And while bored and uncomfortable at times, I resolved to have similar experiences close to nature in the life that lay ahead of me.

SAN FRANCISCO, CALIFORNIA

In 1961, I went to San Francisco. My mother refused to fly, so we took the train everywhere. She agreed to travel by air only by the late 1960s, after an agonizing trip to Boston on the rails. We came from Chicago via Los Angeles, staying at the historic Palace Hotel near the train station on Market Street. My dad flew out later to attend a convention. As was always the case, I was allowed to venture away from the hotel on my own to explore the city. On a particular outing, I saw a couple sitting in a truck on Market Street. She was white, blonde, and pretty, and he was black. They were having a heated verbal exchange. Oblivious to their surroundings, the argument continued for quite a while. Somehow their exchanges mesmerized me. After some time, their words abruptly stopped and they kissed. Obviously, the event was one I've never forgotten. For me, it carries an important set of associations that I likely couldn't immediately articulate. But later, I could see that the associations contained diversity, openness, conflict, resolution, and hopefully, love. I understood the potential that there, in San Francisco, was a world where all things were possible.

Evanston was a diverse community with good schools. But prior to college, my learning was general and with little depth of knowledge. At Berkeley in 1969, I was suddenly thrown into a larger and more radical social environment, a lot of which was a large, messy experiment. The conflicts of the Vietnam War, the openness of California, and the new developments in food and domestic living made for a time of dramatic changes. Nothing was dull from the moment I arrived in Berkeley—from the protests in People's Park to 1974, when Patty Hearst was kidnapped—also the year of my departure.

The environment of California at that time always challenged my preconceived assumptions. I remember going to a concert given by Miles Davis at Royce Hall on the UCLA campus in Los Angeles the following year—1970—at a moment when a major shift in his musical sensibility became apparent. The audience was largely black, and many wore Afros, and were decked out in colorful dashikis and elaborate headscarves. A woman came up on the stage to introduce the performers. She spoke to the audience and said something I've never forgotten: "To the few white people in the audience tonight, it's not that we choose to exclude you, it's just that we choose to ignore you." Her remarks were riveting.

I've always tried to hold onto that awareness of what it means to be white, male, and upper middle class, all the advantages one has, and all that one takes for granted as a result. So for many years, I sought out diversity. I heard Angela Davis speak, and Jean Genet discourse curiously in French. Even though I think Genet had quite a good command of English, his talk was translated by a Black Panther on stage. So much of the emphasis at that time was on alienation, which magnified the impact of such events. It was definitely another place.

At Berkeley, I came under the influence of various architects, including William Turnbull, Jr., Charles Moore, and Joseph Esherick, who had all taught there. They represented a specific and fresh design aesthetic, which had come from Modernism but also contained a vernacular sensibility in response to the particular environment of the San Francisco Bay Area. Their homes were small, the planning was open, and the materials were typically chosen for their availability and sensuousness. They were straightforward and unadorned. I enjoyed their simplicity and intimacy tremendously. I always note the diverging sensibilities between buildings that are cool, abstract, and impersonal, and homes that are warmer, potentially more vernacular, and intimate.

Richard Whitaker, Donlyn Lyndon, Charles Moore, and William Turnbull, Jr. at the Sea Ranch, California.

Two other professors who informed my studies were the architect Christopher Alexander, who was noted for his theories about design, and Roger Montgomery, the city planner, architect, and designer. Both were humanists. In collaboration with other colleagues, Alexander had developed an important theory, a "pattern language" that allowed lay people to build in an appropriate vernacular, and Montgomery was noted for his sensitive thinking in urban design. Another academic who was influential was the French-born J.B. Jackson, who was also a writer and an instructor in landscape design, and who taught at Harvard in alternating semesters. Jackson was among the early champions of the diversity of the American rural and urban landscape. I also studied with the German-born Horst Rittel, who influenced design practice. Rittel was a professor, but more importantly, a theoretician. He worked with the United Nations, but also taught at Berkeley. His thesis was a subject called the "wicked problem." Simply put, Rittel would point out that you can gather all the information you can and study it at length, but you cannot avoid making a decision. That pragmatism was very critical. That's what the design process is about. Of course it's ironic now that we're in a time where decision-making is still difficult in spite of the volumes of information readily available. His prophecy has come to be.

A Pattern Language: Towns, Buildings, Construction by Christopher Alexander.

During this period, I never attempted to rationalize or organize all of these divergent ideas. I was content to leave my thinking incomplete, messy, and unresolved, in the realm where enjoyment lies—the best that education affords. I never looked at my school as something I was going to retool and put into a career. Rather, I studied what I enjoyed and found pleasure in, while working hard. I got good grades, but I never tried to foster the type of professionalism seen in students today. There was also a reverse snobbism that existed in my academic environs and the rebellious social world. There was an indifference to achievement and success, even though one was capable of both and extremely sensitive that they were not available.

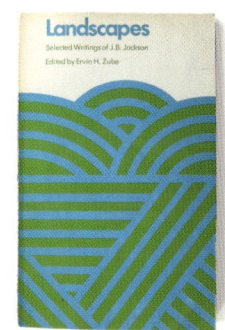
Landscapes by J.B. Jackson.

Berkeley was where I started my pilgrimages. This is what all architects do when they visit houses or locations of renown. An early visit was to the Temple of Wings in the hills of north Berkeley that was renowned because San Francisco native Isadora Duncan danced there. The Temple of Wings was an experimental house comprising an enclosed peristyle of 34 Corinthian columns cast in concrete. Originally designed by the architect Bernard Maybeck and completed by A. Randolph Monroe in 1911, the house and dance studio were commissioned by the owner, Florence Treadwell Boynton,

The colonnades of the Temple of Wings in Berkeley.

The Joseph Esherick House at the Sea Ranch.

Interior of Joe Allen's restaurant on West 46th Street in New York.

Ruby Wax, on Lake Shore Drive in Chicago, 1974.

Gund Hall, at the Harvard Graduate School of Design, by architect John Andrews.

who desired a Greek temple in which her family could dance in the manner of her mentor—none other than Isadora Duncan.

Setting out one morning, Kitty McGraw Berry, a good friend, and I headed to the hill dubbed by a local newspaper "Nut Hill," so named for the nuts and dried fruit diet to which the owners adhered and that was home to the Temple of Wings. We weren't scared by the overgrown landscape that made the temple all the harder to find. We came into the open-air peristyle with its two enclosed areas—one to the left and one to the right in a symmetrical composition—and then we walked into the garden and encountered a lone woman. We asked to see the house and she responded, "Certainly, but you have to help me with something." We said, "Of course." She pointed to a pair of shovels and told us to start digging a ditch. We worked for several hours and were rewarded by being able to walk to the house and enjoy at our leisure all of its artistic elements.

These early pilgrimages were very spontaneous and formative. On another, I went north from Berkeley to Sonoma County to track down a friend who had spent the weekend there. We caught up with each other at the place where he was to live for the next few days, a burned-out redwood tree that he had literally turned into a tree house. A couple of hippies had found a way to make something truly beautiful out of nothing. Later that day, we stopped at the planned community of Sea Ranch, then under construction, and noted all the small and particular houses (as well as those yet to be built) by Moore, Turnbull, and Esherick. The wonderful thing in those days was that you could be totally carefree, show up somewhere and, surprisingly, get in to see an exceptional piece of design on a personal and direct level.

NEW YORK, NEW YORK

After Berkeley, I spent a year knocking around New York. It was a tough, hard time. There was no work to be had anywhere and the harsh indifference of New York was a powerful contrast to the warm and happy embrace of San Francisco. Still, New York's aura was potent. Youth and beauty were magnets for all kinds of opportunity, but there was just nothing one could make money from or live off. The city seemed small and there were only a handful of places to go to. At the time, people were far more accessible, and there would easily be dinners at Joe Allen's with the likes of Thomas Hoving or Tennessee Williams, in the company of the actress Candy Darling. At the encouragement of Rodger Montgomery to continue my education, I applied to the Harvard Graduate School of Design (GSD) in Cambridge, Massachusetts. Surprised when I got in that spring, I left New York and returned to Chicago for the summer and worked as a waiter. Often, I was joined by my old friend and cohort, Ruby Wax. We continued our spontaneous adventures, and at the same time I unabashedly explored my sex life with happy abandon.

THE GROPIUS HOUSE, LINCOLN, MASSACHUSETTS

If Berkeley was pliant, sensuous, and open-minded, Harvard was cold, directed, and focused. Evidence of this was in place from the get-go. On Day One, my class left the campus by bus on a carefully organized trip to visit the wonderful Gropius House in nearby Lincoln, Massachusetts. Designed and built in 1938 by the Bauhaus architect Walter Gropius, who had escaped Nazi Germany, moving first to Great Britain, and then

ROSS ANDERSON   **FREDERIC SCHWARTZ**   **SUSAN MONACIN**   **ALAN WANZENBERG**

Newport, Rhode Island, while at Harvard's GSD.

The Gropius House in Lincoln, Massachusetts.

The dining area in the Gropius House.

Detail of Andrew Melville Hall at St. Andrews University, Scotland, by James Stirling.

Boston City Hall by Kallman, McKinnell and Knowlers, Boston.

to the United States. The outing and accompanying reception were a longstanding tradition for each entering class. Upon arrival, we were told to sit on the floor. Mrs. Gropius then spoke to us and talked about the legacy and the history of the Harvard Graduate School of Design, as well as that of her husband.

The house, remarkably simple and modest, is a great International Modernism building punctuated in every detail, from the way in which the furniture was built-in, to the scale and lines of the house, to the flat roofs and windows specified by function. While one window was designed for viewing, another was designed for ventilation. The visit was an honor, and also interesting to me because of several noteworthy observations I made that were foreign to the architecture of the house. Like European women of her generation, Mrs. Gropius had a dainty dressing table surrounded with eyelet embroidery and adorned with a little skirt and valance. The delicate table was so contrary to the severe International Style architecture in which it sat. Then, in another striking departure from the controlled surrounds of the house, the walls of the daughter's room were covered with posters of James Dean in his defining youth.

The next day, our class sat in a room where the administration spoke of how exactly we'd each been chosen and that henceforth competition between us should cease, and that we should share and collaborate in our academic endeavors. Specific grades would be abandoned in favor of a pass/fail system. It was not exactly the lecture given at the law and business schools to the incoming class ("Look to your left and right…by the end of the first year, one of you will be gone") but it was no doubt heartfelt. Still, I found it hard to believe people highly trained to compete and prevail could change so quickly. We didn't.

Finishing school, that's how I often remember my experience at the GSD: Learning the correct gestures, responses, and methods to employ, reading the right books, and studying the right architects. Elitist and mandarin. It sounds like a complaint, but it's not. Thankfully I had had chaotic and messy Berkeley, so the order and structure at the GSD were of enormous benefit. Harvard was where I learned to work—and work really hard. Every studio's impetus was the juried reviews. All the usual suspects showed up to partake, including the New York Five—Peter Eisenman, Michael Graves, Charles Gwathmey, John Hejduk, and Richard Meier—Robert A.M. Stern, and the Krier Brothers. They were lively, demanding affairs that required weeks of preparation for a short, possibly ten-minute focused presentation with lots of grandstanding by the jurors, mainly for their mutual benefit and their clever sayings. The experiences were memorable, irksome, and rarely led to much, specifically, but rather they offered knowledge of the process for success in the larger world. I did them, but with dismay. Never an acolyte, I didn't want to lose my independence and freedom to think about what I wanted. Nonetheless, the experience challenged me creatively.

There were a few exceptions to this procedure. One was a jury review I had with the Scottish architect James Stirling, who was a guest of the architectural theorist and urbanist Colin Rowe. Stirling presented himself in the most humble and modest way, taking time to comment on any element, and letting his humanistic sensibility show through. He was one of the few jurors who took time to talk to the students. The other was with the German-born American architect, Gerhard Kallmann. His clarity of thought and deep social sensibilities were formative to me. He was the same age as my father, and like my father, had been born in Berlin, albeit to very different circumstances. Kallmann was avuncular and showed little interest in trends or social acceptance, similarly to my mother. And so over the course of my term, Kallmann came to be a wonderful mentor and friend. I was also fortunate to know the architect Ben Thompson, founder of Design Research, who persuaded Walter Gropius to establish the Architects' Collaborative in Cambridge, along with six other colleagues. I was lucky to work in Thompson's firm during my first summer at GSD, serving in a myriad of roles, from the mailroom to the design table. The firm was at a curious moment. Thompson had taken on several jobs in Arab countries, work that had proven to be very challenging and difficult. I remember having an early awareness of how corporate architects can rely too much on work in foreign countries without fully recognizing the cultural challenges that affect the success of their work. To counter this taxing aspect of the firm's portfolio, Thompson, in tandem with the developer The Rouse Company, became immersed in the new concept of the festival marketplace as expressed in the renovation of Boston's Quincy Market as the focal point of the Faneuil Hall Marketplace. The genesis of this radical mixed-use concept is laid out in Thompson's 1966 essay *Visual Squalor and Social Disorder*, in which he argued for city architecture that would encourage, rather than discourage, joy and social life. Today, Thompson would be a lifestyle leader or guru in the marriage of quality of life and design.

FURTHER PILGRIMAGES

FIRST CHURCH OF CHRIST, SCIENTIST, BERKELEY, CALIFORNIA

The church, right in the heart of Berkeley, was two blocks from where I lived. It is an exquisite building that epitomizes the imagination and architectural genius of its designer, Bernard Maybeck, and is truly one of the most stunning structures I've ever seen. You can look at a building and see if its idea has been realized or not. Sometimes it has, but at the cost of poor construction or some other fault. But this church is an example of a fully realized idea that has stood the test of time, with its combination of Oriental, Classical, Romanesque, and Gothic motifs, and its use of integrated industrial materials in a way never done before.

What I thought was so amazing about the church was the workmanship—the notion of building something in the service of God with a beautiful polychromy—and decorating architectural elements in a variety of colors. That kind of craftsmanship is the highest of human ability and the building is absolutely extraordinary. Few people know that Maybeck was a mystic, even though it's so evident in this architecture. What I observed and learned from Maybeck's attention to detail and craftsmanship in this church has resonated with me throughout my career.

LE CORBUSIER, SWITZERLAND, AND FRANCE

When I was 23, I went to Europe and visited the Le Corbusier buildings in Switzerland, as well as those in France, such as the Villa Fallet in La Chaux-de-Fonds and the Nôtre Dame du Haut chapel in Ronchamp. In Geneva, I saw the Immeuble Clarté, an apartment building Corbusier designed, that was a smaller version of his Unité d'Habitation in Marseilles. During the same trip, I also went to Italy—to Florence,

Design Research logo.

Quincy Market and Faneuil Hall, Boston.

Interior of First Church of Christ, Scientist, Berkeley.

Le Corbusier's Nôtre Dame du Haut chapel in Ronchamp.

The Walter Fisher House in Hubbard Woods, Illinois.

Interior of the Fisher House, mid-1930s.

The staircase at the Fisher House.

View of the Glass House from the ravine on the property.

San Gimignano, the famous walled medieval hill town in Tuscany, Venice, and to several Palladian buildings near Vicenza. Pilgrimages to certain sites were fundamental and necessary to my training and understanding of architecture.

THE WALTER FISHER HOUSE, HUBBARD WOODS, ILLINOIS

During the summers of the two years I was studying at Harvard, I worked in Chicago at the firm of Booth, Nagle & Hartray. One of my office colleagues was Nancy Bush, who grew up in her family's exceptional house in Chicago, known as the Walter Fisher House, which she said I had to see. The house was situated in a quiet neighborhood on the North Shore, graced by an immensely tall tree canopy indigenous to the area. It had been designed by Howard Fisher in 1928 for his brother Walter Fisher, while Howard was a student at the Harvard School of Design. Their father was the prominent Chicago lawyer and conservationist Walter L. Fisher, who had risen to national status as Secretary of the Interior under President William Howard Taft. Ironically, Howard, who went on to become the founder and director of the GSD Laboratory of Computer Graphics from 1964 to 1974, had retired just as I had arrived at the school. I knew of him but only from a distance. Walter Fisher had hired his brother to design a Prairie-style house melded with the International Style, which Howard Fisher accomplished in a masterful way. The aesthetics and features of the house profoundly affected my sensibilities. The living room was exceptionally well proportioned. The dining room was complemented in the most soothing way by the shape and elevation of its windows, creating an intimacy for conversation and dining pleasure. With my visual memory of Castle Park, I was struck by the immense open porch on the roof as well as by the nearby outdoor fireplace as spaces that call for socializing. And as if the open porch were not enough, the house also has a spacious open sundeck on the roof.

The Fisher House is a place where I came to understand the aesthetics of the staircase beyond its functionality. Here, it fulfills its role as an element through which the aesthetic details of the house culminate and focus on the sensibility of the dwelling. The simple gesture of the slight curves in the stair rails are sublime, and the height of the risers is perfectly scaled to the pitch of the stairway itself.

THE GLASS HOUSE, NEW CANAAN, CONNECTICUT

When I was young, I always loved utopian houses, as they had a certain perfection to them. In the mid-1970s, I had the occasion to visit another utopian house, the Glass House by Philip Johnson, with fellow graduate student, Tarek Ashkar, who was doing a term paper at Harvard's Fogg Museum on the recently opened sculpture gallery at the complex. At the time, one could write to Johnson directly and simply ask, "May I come and visit your house?" Tarek had arranged to go and asked if I wanted to come along.

We spent an entire day there. I remember the caretaker approaching us, opening the doors to the buildings, saying, "Enjoy yourself," and then leaving us alone. The December day was mostly gray and overcast. The house, I thought, was more interesting at that time of year. At one point, snow started falling, and I realized how intimate yet also heroic the house was. The intimacy was the scale of the building and its heroic nature, the building's setting and materials, and the way in which the house braved the elements. The site of the house is in a part of Connecticut that is very

SCULPTURE GALLERY AT THE GLASS HOUSE

From the left, Andy Warhol, David Whitney, Philip Johnson, Dr. John Dalton, and Robert A.M. Stern at the Glass House, 1964.

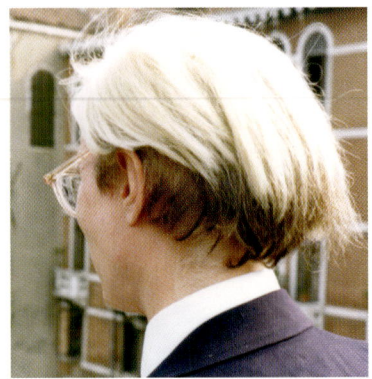

Andy Warhol in Venice, Italy, 1980.

President John F. Kennedy's desk, with his PT-109 coconut, right, at the John F. Kennedy Presidential Library and Museum, Boston.

The Portland Museum of Art, Portland, Maine, designed by Henry N. Cobb.

beautiful. I always think about how people in New England built houses along the shore with tiny windows, steeling themselves against harsh weather. The Glass House was just the opposite. It opened itself up to the elements, partly through the technology Johnson leveraged in its design. That day, a large bowl of lemons was prominent in the main room. There must have been 20 of them in a bowl on the countertop, with really nothing else in the house—no magazines, newspapers, or other objects sitting around. The lemons looked theatrical to me. What I thought was interesting about the huge bowl of lemons was that their presence was purely for visual pleasure. Who's going to eat 20 lemons? But I would remember this bowl of lemons so specifically and their color against the grayness of the day.

It was intriguing to consider the myth and then the truth of the Glass House, or the image one imagines and then the reality—like the baldish Andy Warhol going out every night, being identified by his hair, and coming home to bed and taking his wig off. Although Johnson and his partner David Whitney didn't really live in the Glass House, the myth that they did is so well established that people exclaim, "What do you mean? They didn't sleep there?" Or "What do you mean? Andy takes a wig off every night?" In fact, Johnson and Whitney spent most of their time in a series of vernacular farmhouses situated above the Glass House. And it was to those that they retired.

I.M. PEI & PARTNERS, NEW YORK

I moved to New York in the fall of 1978 and got a job at I.M. Pei & Partners through an obscure connection at the GSD. As I learned at the time, most roads emanate from Harvard. I was one of only a handful of new hires. Pei's was an earnest, intelligent, and very hard-working environment.

The salaries were low, even though the firm had terrific commissions. During my first year, I was paid $6,500. And one could be focused for weeks on end on the most esoteric of details. I remember working on the John F. Kennedy Presidential Library and Museum, which was about to open in Boston. I was doing an endless number of drawings of President Kennedy's desk at the White House, on which he kept a coconut that survived the sinking of his PT-109 during World War II. For the museum display, it had to be attached somehow to the desk and held in place. To me, this project was like the sublime and the absurd—in Pei's renowned office, I ended up studying the most obscure details.

Ideas abounded and were discussed in specifics often driven by pre-established geometries that emphasized proportion, scale, and rhythm. Every salient element was prioritized as to its value, and design battles were very hard-fought. The firm had an unspoken dress code and held expectations of intense personal commitment to the work at hand. I loved it. Over my first two years, I racked up almost 2,000 hours of (unpaid) overtime. The experience provided great discipline, especially after the fallow years of work that had preceded it. It was a very congenial environment. Regardless of your respective title and work on a project, the firm was resolute to see that you were acknowledged in any and all types of publicity. So I've always been listed on the design team for the Portland Museum of Fine Arts, in Portland, Maine, an evocative building done by Henry Cobb, one of the founding partners of I.M. Pei & Partners. Cobb was cerebral, and the museum building is really his study on Louis Kahn's Library at Phillips Exeter Academy in Exeter, New Hampshire. I next joined the team engaged with the design of New York's Jacob K. Javits Convention Center, headed by Pei himself and the German-born James Freed.

While working there, I lived with a group of guys and my boyfriend, Stephen Webster, in a sixth-floor walk-up loft. It was a very loose social environment with a lot of comings and goings. People were selfish, and the experience could have been a precursor to a gay version of the television series *Friends*. In 1978, New York was prescient, dirty, raucous, accessible, and creative.

JED JOHNSON

I met Jed in the spring of 1980. A mutual friend, the Swiss art dealer Thomas Ammann, made the introduction, telling us both that "we'd have a lot in common." Occasionally, and at Thomas' suggestion, I would leave work at the I.M. Pei offices and go to one of the lunches held regularly at the Factory, Andy Warhol's studio—lively affairs that were well attended by people largely in business, in the entertainment industry, and the sports world. My first meeting with Jed was brief and distracting, given the clamorous setting. Jed was handsome and neatly dressed, shy, and soft-spoken. And indeed, we had a lot in common. My clearest memory of seeing Jed the next time was running into him on Madison Avenue near Saint Patrick's Cathedral later that spring. In that chance encounter, we spoke at some length, standing in the middle of the sidewalk, and resolved to get together soon.

Not long after, Jed asked me to swing by Andy's townhouse where he and Andy lived. I had been there once before, for Thanksgiving dinner, before meeting Jed. Andy had invited Thomas, who in turn invited me. Catherine Guinness and Bob Colacello were also there. The most memorable and longest part of the evening was the group sitting in the kitchen eating turkey with Andy's maids, Nena and Aurora. Andy's two dachshunds, Archie and Amos, barked through the entire meal, and the television was blaring the entire time for no particular reason, as no one was watching it. I remember that the phone rang and it was Jed calling from Vail, Colorado, and that he and Andy spoke briefly. Later, Thomas told me Andy was paranoid about letting anyone come to the house. Even Bob, considering all his years at the Factory, had never been to the house until then, and so my visit with Thomas was very unusual.

My subsequent invitation to the townhouse was different in nature. This time, Jed gave me an extended tour through the various rooms he was decorating. The building was a brick and limestone Georgian Revival four-story, four-bedroom home in solid condition, with all its original details intact, and where Andy lived as discretely as he could. The place was elegantly detailed and elaborate, in a way I'd not seen before. It was fastidious in an obsessive way. The townhouse was not only home to Jed and Andy, but to Andy's myriad objects, paintings, and his more iconic pieces of furniture that ranged from American to Americana to Art Deco. Everywhere were dozens of unpacked bags filled with purchases that remained largely as they were when Andy first brought them home. I left quite amazed.

Soon, Jed and I began spending a tremendous amount of time with each other and our relationship evolved quickly into an intense friendship. We shared much in common from our Midwestern backgrounds, from the pleasure in work and activity, to a love of design in an inclusive, non-scholarly way. However, both of us were living with others.

The Jacob K. Javits Convention Center by James Ingo Freed of I.M. Pei & Partners, New York.

Stephen Webster, left, and Alan, in New York on the Hudson River, 1978.

Jed in Central Park, New York, 1981.

Andy Warhol, left, and Alan, in New York, around 1979.

Fred Hughes in the Mediterranean, around 1980.

The living room in Christiane Schlumberger's apartment, New York, around 1983.

The interior of Mick Jagger's townhouse on the Upper West side of Manhattan, mid-1980s.

Sushi furniture designed by Jane Millet, for Stargroves on Mustique.

But as Jed and I collaborated more on his early design commissions, the four of us—Jed, Andy, my boyfriend Stephen Webster, and I—started to spend time together.

Although I did not comprehend all of Jed's history when first we met, it soon became clear that he was struggling for his independence from Andy. As I gradually learned, Jed had hoped for a complete relationship, but Andy was incapable of mentoring and partnering in their shared activities, particularly in the movies Jed worked on. Jed was tethered and reluctant to leave a situation of tremendous comfort and security but that was emotionally barren. My impression was that for Jed to grow and really become the person he wanted to be, he needed to get out of the relationship. Jed and I were not involved at that point, but I was direct with him in my attempts to build his confidence. Jed recognized his various talents. After many months, an emotional relationship between us eventually happened, and at that point, we resolved to leave our mutual situations and to begin a life together.

OUR FIRST COMMISSION

By the spring of 1981, I had left my job at I.M. Pei. Jed and I were working together, running a business we had started out of our apartment on West 67th Street.

Andy's business manager, Fred Hughes, grew up in Houston's Fair Oaks and was mentored by John and Dominique de Menil, the Texas-based family of art philanthropists who had played a key role in his life and career. Fred recommended us to Christiane Schlumberger and Katie Jones, Dominique's nieces. Modest and reserved, both women possessed a sophisticated elegance that came from their family life, as well as from the combination of having grown up in Houston, the big dynamic Texas oil town, and living in France, with its deep culture and quiet refinements. During a summer in the late 1980s, I remember visiting Christiane at her family home in Tourtour, a village above Vence in southeastern France. The modern French farmhouse had a wonderful, unpretentious rusticity. The house was done in a sophisticated sensibility, wth Persian carpets and modern art. Christiane provided Jed and me with an important early commission to redesign the small, intimate space of a penthouse that she owned around the corner from our apartment in New York. The result was a highly detailed design that showed an early sensibility on our part to create a unified whole—in this case, the unusual fusion of French Art Deco with American Arts & Crafts.

MUSTIQUE, THE GRENADINES

At the suggestion of Fred Hughes, Mick Jagger contacted us. He wanted us to work on a townhouse he had purchased on West 81st Street. It was partially constructed with a design initiated by others. We got on board and rationalized our plan to work hard to make up for lost time, saving and correcting the work that had been done and inserting new elements that appealed to Mick's design sense. This work was done during the years immediately following the shooting of John Lennon, which drove me to become highly sensitive to the demand for privacy and safety that we all require, but that are particularly critical to celebrities. I was impressed by Mick's straightforwardness and desire for things to be "attractive but robust." His life was instilled with surprisingly substantial values, demonstrated by a tremendous focus on his career and extended family. Mick managed his fame well. He kept things uncomplicated whenever possible. Extremely well-educated and knowledgeable about history, he also possessed a strong visual acuity. He had been exposed to many things by the influential antiques dealer Christopher Gibbs, among others. He made his own telephone calls, carried his own luggage, and I thought he was remarkable in his ability to relax and ratchet things down. This early insight into celebrity life was valuable for me. I became aware that fame could be controlled—it doesn't have to control the person.

The success of our New York endeavor for Mick led to working on Stargroves, his Caribbean home on Mustique Island in the Grenadines. This was a job that went on for nearly ten years, exposing me to this area of the world and to Mustique in particular.

Mustique had been developed in the 1970s by the Scottish Colin Tennant, better known as Lord Glenconnor, who was a great modern eccentric. He had the wisdom to retain the talented and imaginative English set designer Oliver Messel to design the initial structures of the compound, which were really small cottages rendered in a marvelous indigenous style typical of the West Indies. The houses were harmonious, well-planned, and oriented with cross ventilation. Tennant first designed the Cotton House, which was a small hotel and restaurant central to the island, and then various small cottages mainly for members of the British upper class. Again, and reminiscent of my early years at Castle Park, Messel used charming and creative names for each, such as Clonsilla, Phibblestown, Seastar, and Blue Waters. Clearly Messel had kept things practical—working with local craftsmen to produce straightforward architectural designs inspired by the indigenous buildings of the Caribbean, and embellishing them with sophisticated details and furnishings. I loved the years I spent working there, the isolation, the natural surrounds, and the unconstructed time I had to absorb these intricate and inventive details.

CONYERS FARM, GREENWICH, CONNECTICUT

At the same time, we became involved in the early design work and planning for Conyers Farm, a substantial old estate property acquired by entrepreneur Peter Brant. Conyers Farm was built on some 1,500 acres of rural land in the early 1900s by the industrialist Edmund Converse, and designed by the well-educated architect Donn Barber, whose training included studies at the Ecole des Beaux-Arts in Paris. Developed as a working farm, Conyers provided substantial quantities of fresh produce to the Greenwich community through the 1920s. After Converse died, the property fell into decline and was eventually sold to Lewis Rosentiel, the multi-millionaire founder of Schenley Industries, who proceeded to abandon many of the extant structures with the intent of building a dense subdivision.

By the time the farm was acquired by Brant, the property was overgrown and the 18 remaining buildings were in disrepair. Early on, and with remarkable thoughtfulness, Peter's wife, Sandra Brant, became focused on the type of architecture that could potentially be built with the intent of creating buildings on large parcels in complementary architectural styles. She, Jed, and I discussed at great length all the marvelous architecture that had been built in the United States by such early twentieth-century designers as David Adler and partners Walter Mellor, Arthur I. Meigs, and George Howe. A particularly influential architect was Harrie T. Lindeberg, as he

Colin Tennant's Great House on Mustique.

A detail of the exterior of Clonsilla, one of Oliver Messel's houses on Mustique.

The Clubhouse at Conyers Farm in Greenwich, Connecticut.

One of the numerous restored outbuildings at Conyers Farm.

Sketch for a house by architect Harrie T. Lindeberg, 1940.

Henryk de Kwiatkowski's house at Conyers Farm.

The dining room at the de Kwiatkowski house, done in collaboration with Parish-Hadley Associates.

Interior of the Robert Venturi house in Vail, early 1980s.

demonstrated a command of various historic styles, a fluidity of detailing, and a unique but conservative taste for experimentation. Our hope was to have guidelines that would promote a similar development in a contemporary subdivision, taking into account that this was one of the first large developments that anticipated the great residential construction booms of the 1980s and 1990s. I became engaged with the abandoned buildings. Early in our discussions, Jed and I had thought a lot about their restoration and reinterpreted functions. Conyers Farm was a laboratory for us, a way to study structures in varying states of decline, and looking at how they could be restored and repurposed in useful ways.

Through the Brants, I was approached by Henryk de Kwiatkowski to do the architectural work on a substantial group of original buildings at Conyers Farm. Henryk, a highly successful aeronautical engineer who later became a world-class thoroughbred horse breeder and polo player, had purchased 100 acres at Conyers Farm, primarily where the abandoned barn—nearly two acres of enclosed space—had been situated. I was ready to approach my work with a host of ideas based on the considerations I had previously given to the property. Though Jed and I were full of energy, the times were lean with actual work, so we welcomed this significant and extensive project.

Soon after my work began as the project architect, Henryk retained Sister Parish, an American interior decorator and socialite—née Dorothy May Kinnicutt—as the decorator. My work with her exposed me to a system of well-organized planning and thinking. I was also able to meet her partner Albert Hadley, who wasn't directly involved with the project but who was kind enough to make himself available on the occasions I felt incapable of discussing my ideas with Sister Parish.

I was highly deferential to Sister Parish, who was from another generation. Though quite demanding, she was, redeemingly, often funny and insightful. What I learned most from her was how to plan a large home, doing justice to the necessary support spaces, such as the laundry room, mudroom, and pantry. Often large homes are laid out with little specificity as to these areas, but Sister Parish had mastered their detailing. Her willingness to educate me, which was not unlike my earlier experience with Mrs. Robertson at the Thorne Miniature Rooms, gave me a deeper knowledge of the complexity of residential layouts.

VAIL, COLORADO

During this period, Jed and I had many quiet achievements. My memories are vivid with the enormous amount of time Jed and I spent together. When two people work and live together, the passage of time creates a density of knowledge, familiarity, and experience in understanding both one's partner as well as oneself for which there is no substitute. Outside of our time together, we socialized in limited ways with a handful of clients and personal friends.

Jed and I retreated as much as we could to Vail, Colorado, where, in the late 1970s, he had built a house designed by Robert Venturi with Peter and Sandra Brant, as Jed and they were very close friends. The house was used very little by the Brants, as Peter became more involved with polo and thoroughbred racing in Florida. So we went to the Venturi house a lot, especially at Thanksgiving, Christmas, and as

ONE OF THE RESTORED PROJECTS ON THE HENRYK DE KWIATKOWSKI PROPERTY, CONYERS FARM

Alan in front of the Robert Venturi house in Vail.

Street scene, New Delhi, India, 1991.

Alan at the Taj Mahal, Agra, India.

Subway graffiti by Keith Baugh, New York, 1973.

often as we could throughout the year. The house, situated on Vail Mountain, was beautifully constructed with materials of great quality. Vail, like our later homes on Water Island, was easily accessible and yet, once one got there, remote and intimate. Both homes placed us less in a social environment and more in a private one in natural surroundings. We could stay at the Vail house for days on end with little contact with others, aside from our time on the slopes, where we were both aggressive skiers. With long periods of unstructured time, Jed and I had the chance to recharge and reflect. The time was also profoundly necessary to establish the foundation of our relationship.

The 1980s were a time of very hard work. By now, both of us were in our thirties, and challenged not only by our design business and our clients but also by New York—the devastation of AIDS and losing many of our friends to the disease—and then by the unprecedented wave of affluence and celebrated "greed," combined with desperate poverty and homelessness.

INDIA

In a spontaneous move inspired by the mileage I had accumulated on Pan Am Airlines from the years of traveling to Mustique, I booked two tickets to India for Jed and myself before the airline folded. Leaving on Christmas Eve of 1990, we had done little to intellectually or emotionally prepare ourselves for the journey. The bellicose times for that region, especially the new border tensions in Kashmir and the inevitable start of the first Gulf War on January 15th, wrought havoc, and forced us to alter our plans, canceling our planned visit to Srinagar.

I remembered I had taken a life-drawing class at Berkeley. The instructor had just returned from India on a Fulbright scholarship. Thinking I'd visit there on a return trip from Pakistan where my uncle had worked as an engineer, I asked how much time I should give to India. She paused and said "a lifetime." While Jed and I had only three weeks on that first trip, we made the most of it and were transformed by the experience. Traveling mostly in Rajasthan, we managed to get to Varanasi on December 30, Jed's birthday, and a day later to Agra, to visit the Taj Mahal in the early morning on the day of our return to New York. The blue moon was still visible as the sun rose. The trip had been explosive, overwhelming us with aesthetics and maturing our sensibilities. Our thinking was now different. We saw events and design in more integrated and magnified ways. The poverty in India was horrific, but at the same time, we witnessed a profound sense of charity and grace.

India was also visually staggering and exhausting. I remember we would go out during the day and then come back to our hotel, where we would just lie in bed looking up at the ceiling in an attempt to quiet down our eyes. As much as India expanded my worldly sensibilities, the country expanded Jed's more to the potential of a future. Jed saw firsthand how he could make interior furnishings by producing his designs with his particular vision. And he saw that opportunity as a way to remove himself from the day-to-day demands of running an interior design business. Jed was always wonderful in the one-on-one relationship with clients, where they really respected his experience and expertise. But the business aspects of the industry always challenged him. Jed wanted to work in design in a way that liberated him from those.

Making and selling things offered just that—a liberation that he later achieved through product development in various textiles, custom-made furniture, and lighting.

HOUSING WORKS, NEW YORK

At the end of the trip, we returned to New York—to the AIDS situation and homelessness—determined to make a difference. So we committed ourselves fully to the nascent project of Housing Works by designing and building a facility for the organization. We had been fortunate to meet three of the four members of the legendary AIDS activist group—Keith Cylar, Charles King, and Eric Sawyer—who had decided to dedicate themselves to serving one of the city's most neglected groups of citizens, the tens of thousands of homeless men, women, and children in New York City living with HIV and AIDS, by starting Housing Works. They believed that stable housing was the key to helping HIV-positive people live healthy and fulfilling lives, as well as the key to preventing the further spread of the virus. Their recognition of housing as a stabilizing social factor resonated with our own beliefs about the importance of a person's dwelling to his or her quality of life. The stalwart commitment of Housing Works to New York drew us to become involved, and we felt honored to contribute through our design work. Ultimately, Jed and I designed and built their flagship residence on East 9th Street over the course of six years, despite tremendous challenges created by government bureaucracy and, in particular, the Giuliani administration.

The entrance to Housing Works, New York, mid-1990s.

One of the rooms in the Housing Works residence.

TWO SEMINAL PROJECTS

By the early 1990s, we had accomplished several significant projects, largely at Conyers Farm, but also in apartments and various remodeling jobs. We also had a few that were only partially realized but contained the elements of larger ideas of our design aesthetic. Then in late 1991, two large, definitive projects came to our firm. One was the luxurious and elegant apartment for Maureen and Marshall Cogan on Fifth Avenue in Manhattan and the other was the whimsical, complex, and sometimes irreverent resort called Twin Farms, located in Barnard, Vermont, a commission from the Thurston Twigg Smith family. Both works were demanding, requiring a virtuosity of talent in combining architecture and interior design into a seamless whole. And both came to us simultaneously after a decade of our working together. The resulting designs resoundingly established our firm.

The Cogan apartment in particular drew on Jed's tremendous skill at assembling furniture and building a spectacular collection of Art Deco pieces for the couple. It also drew heavily on the detailing that we had been developing together in our architectural vocabulary. Although it was not a large apartment and had a wonderful intimacy, it was very thorough and complete in all its details. Twin Farms, on the other hand, drew on my design experiences and time at Castle Park, as well as the subsequent influences of the years in the Caribbean, seeing the work of Oliver Messel. Jed and I knew immediately that Twin Farms needed a quiet exterior with fairly sophisticated, humorous, and elaborate interiors. Both commissions were based heavily on our experiences, our visual memories, and the ability to execute designs exceptionally well. Jed and I had established a practice where we were capable of

The library in Marshall and Maureen Cogan's apartment, New York, around 1993.

Exterior of one of the numerous cottages at Twin Farms, in Barnard, Vermont, around 1995.

TWIN FARMS, BARNARD, VERMONT

MAUREEN AND MARSHALL COGAN
APARTMENT, NEW YORK

Inventive use of birch in a bedroom at Twin Farms.

Jed, between Alan and Gus, on Water Island, Spring, 1996.

Alan, left, and Jed at Philip Johnson's birthday party at the Museum of Modern Art, New York, July, 1996.

Jed, left, and Alan on Water Island, mid-1990s.

reinventing historic interiors in a contemporary and fresh way, encompassing the architectural detailing, furniture, décor, and comfort of each of these residences.

MOVING ON

Since Andy's death in 1987, and after the myriad contents of his private life ended up in a wildly successful estate sale at Sotheby's, a brighter light shone on Jed. He was finally acknowledged, in particular by Fred Hughes, for his numerous accomplishments in the creation of Andy's private world. Andy's death had liberated Jed and allowed him to embrace his talents and potential. This was especially poignant knowing Jed's struggles during the years he lived with Andy. Jed was a thoughtful, quiet man in a noisy and loud world. His achievements were unique, as he was self-taught and always relied on his visual intuition. He had never worked with a prominent designer or in a large firm, and considered his years at the Warhol factory as his education. The broad acknowledgment of the varied and often virtuosic designs that our firm created in commissions from the early 1990s brought success on many levels, and projects—from some of the most prominent collectors in New York—were abundant. We had transitioned from a youthful firm with an inchoate sensibility into a mature company with a strong and capable organization and an aesthetic penchant for the varied, the authentic, and the unexpected. Our hallmark was the ability to coordinate the interiors and the architecture into simple but sophisticated designs that were devoid of pretension. This achievement had an important influence on our personal lives. We were emotionally comfortable and had matured into a partnership that embraced all that we had in common, accepted those few areas where we differed, and sustained a deep passion for each other. By the time of his death in July of 1996, Jed was possibly the happiest I had known him, for he had finally become the man he had always striven to be.

After Jed's death, I was fortunate enough to have a lot of work, most of it from prior clients. I stayed close to home and spent long periods of time in my apartment and on Water Island. A year passed before I traveled extensively. Ironically, the first trip I took was to Paris, and it was both invigorating and terribly nostalgic. I felt my first inclinations to furnish and decorate beyond the limited involvement I had had when Jed was alive.

Subsequently, visiting Paris five or six times a year, and getting to know a select group of furniture dealers, turned into a wonderful adventure and provided me with a solid education of the world of antiques and decoration.

THE NORMAN TOWNHOUSE

In 1941, the artist, social activist, and patron Dorothy Norman and her ex-husband, Edward Norman, commissioned an International Style house designed by the Swiss-born and educated, American architect William Lescaze. Best known for the groundbreaking PSFS Building, a 1930s office tower in Philadelphia, when he was in partnership with George Howe, Lescaze was a singular practitioner of the International Style, specifically in the construction of private homes in New York. The Norman townhouse, with its glazed white brick and glass block exterior, was an exceptional example. When it came on the market, after Mrs. Norman's death in 1997, numerous architectural groups held receptions at the house, which I was unable to attend. I asked my friend, real estate broker MacRae Parker, to arrange a private walk-through for me, as if I were a prospective buyer. It was a powerful experience. The house had been little changed since the day it was built. I eventually confessed that I was not a buyer but simply a very curious architect. After a sympathetic exchange, the realtor indicated that no one was interested in purchasing the house, and that whoever would buy it would most likely tear it down. I was dismayed. Then, by total coincidence, an old friend of mine bought it. It was a perfect resolution. She asked me to work on it, and we went through a rigorous and thoughtful restoration of the house, looking at the archival materials that Lescaze had donated to Syracuse University. The result was an homage to Norman and Lescaze, as well as the opportunity to retain a unique piece of New York residential history.

HOUSE IN SYDNEY

In 1998, I received an interesting commission to work on an historic, landmarked house in the eastern suburbs of Sydney, Australia, for a young, active, Australian family that had lived in America for many years. My client wanted to relocate his widowed father, a Holocaust survivor, back to Sydney. As a gesture to his wife's fondness for America, he offered to hire an American architect, so that she would have an ongoing connection to the place that she had grown to love. The house had been remodeled many times, as there had been no appreciation for many of the historical buildings in Sydney. This commission was to occupy me for the next five years. I loved Sydney and the Australians, as I found them to be engaging, knowledgeable, and completely unaffected. Most Australians, in their youth, travel around the world, absorbing a mix of ideas and influences, which has made for fascinating examples in architecture, fashion, and especially food. I was reminded of the beach life that I had known in Chicago and California, as well as the sensibility of Berkeley in the 1970s. We worked exhaustively on the interiors, bringing in examples of Art Deco as well as pieces by French designer Jean Royère. One of my fondest memories was the association we had with another architect, Hungarian by birth, and who had emigrated to Australia after World War II. A Holocaust survivor, he had been one of 26 boys rounded up by the Nazis and put into a work camp. Miraculously, he and all his classmates survived. Given my own circumstances, this story was compelling and gave me an example of survival and moving on that I will never forget, coming from a quiet man who perceived the world with pleasure and gratefulness.

KETCHUM, IDAHO

Another significant commission at the time was the design of a compound for a New York family in Ketchum, Idaho, on a 60-acre tract of land along the Big Wood River. I was inspired by the numerous structures that had been built by the federal government in our national parks during the first half of the twentieth century. The commission also drew me back to the early lessons in planning projects on the scope of Conyers Farm. It was an opportunity for me to be in close contact with nature. While Jed and I used to go to the mountains together, this was a new location, one that I had not been to before with him, so I could experience it in an original way. I would get out there, work hard, and then go hiking or skiing, connecting with what I believe to be the most basic and fundamental things. The five-year project eventually included building a house, a guesthouse, a caretaker's cottage, various outbuildings, and numerous landscape elements, all done in a Western ranch–vernacular style.

The facade of the 1941 Norman House by William Lescaze, New York.

The restoration by Alan of the living room of the Norman townhouse.

Exterior veranda house in Sydney that Alan worked on.

House in Ketchum, Idaho, designed by Alan.

2 DESTINATIONS: TEN PROJECTS

...that lead to an extended creative endeavor, resulting in the making of notable places and distinctive objects.

A.M. Cassandre poster of the Normandie is from 1938.

HIGH CEILINGS AND EXOTIC WOODS FOR A NEW YORK DUPLEX

The great interior designer Albert Hadley once said that designing a home is really about coming to grips with who you are, what you love, what you aspire to, what you wish to wake up to every day, and what you want to live with. This simple statement is inspirational, and I think about it a lot in my work. Hadley is describing a process that can arc in time over not just the duration of a project, but really over one's lifetime, in terms of aesthetic engagement. Saying this requires self-knowledge and an openness to new ideas. It is my belief that the design process should be more than enjoyable: It should be stimulat-

> **It is my belief that the design process should be more than enjoyable. It should be stimulating and memorable.**

ing and memorable, and by the time one is done with it, the client will have an intimate knowledge of the design. This is not easy, nor is it for everybody. In this home, the clients were active participants, and were confident enough to discuss areas of their general interest with me, and then let me present them with different concepts of design and art that resulted in the finished project. And because of their diverse professions and backgrounds, they had an enterprising point of view. So we looked at different kinds of art, such as Abstract Expressionism, Chinese Export paintings, and early American Modernism. A large, antique Japanese screen in the dining room offers a counterpoint to the view of the river, a panorama that is controlled and more serene. In the kitchen, we used pieces by Robert Mouseman Thompson, the British furniture maker. With its subtle humor, the cabinet has both a sturdiness and a well-crafted quality. However, my favorite of the pieces we acquired is the Italian Renaissance mantelpiece in the living room, with its marvelous and intricate detailing. It is small and complex, but with an overscaled mirror above, and eighteenth-century Dutch glass sconces on each side, the composition grows in scale and impact. As always, I wanted to select items that are beautifully crafted. Two wonderful pale-green upholstered Jean-Michel Frank armchairs, and a marvelous pair of lamps flanking the living room sofa, not only add to the overall feeling of confidence, but complete the eclectic mix—a great combination of things brought back from the clients travels and family heirlooms. In that sense, the interior represents not just a physical journey, but also one that travels through various aesthetic periods. We made things bigger, in scale with the proportions of the high ceilings. I felt that more traditional proportions would be a little too modest. We also incorporated tropical woods, such as Afrormosia and Anigre, which are produced in Africa. In the library, I used a veneer-like wallpaper, and applied paneling to the walls to give the room more of a contemporary feel. When it came to the furnishings, I opted to use the best examples of more traditional pieces because I felt they would ground the apartment.

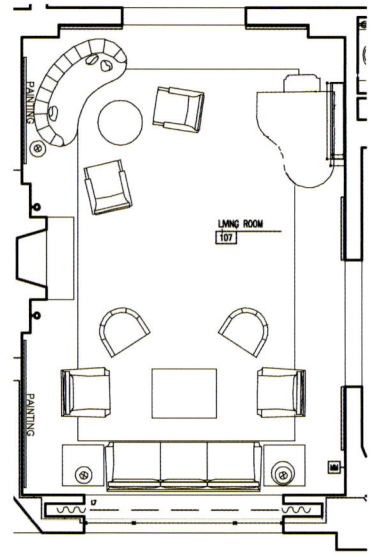

The large living room has two seating areas, on either side of the fireplace.

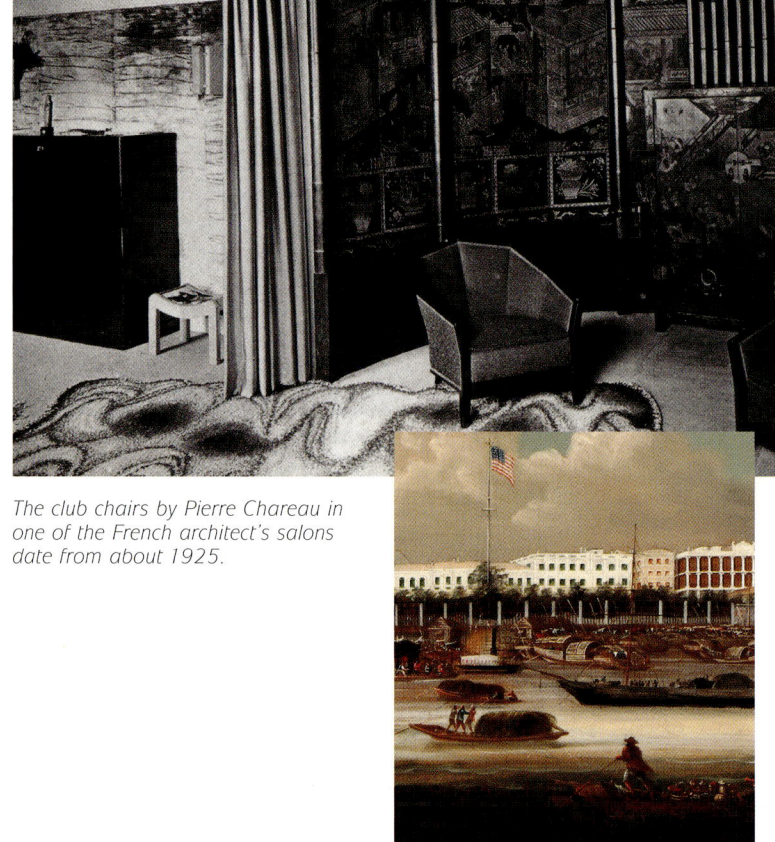

The club chairs by Pierre Chareau in one of the French architect's salons date from about 1925.

A detail from a nineteenth-century China Trade School painting depicts the Waterfront Hongs in Canton, China.

LIGHTING

In the early 1980s, I put together an extensive collection of turn-of–the-twentieth century lighting, mainly inspired by the Arts & Crafts fixtures by such designers as W.A.S. Benson and Gustav Stickley. These were decorative, transitional pieces to accommodate the change in the source of lighting from gas to electricity. With gas lighting, the arm of the sconce turned upward for safety reasons, but with electrical lighting came the lightbulb. With its heating element encased in glass, the lightbulb could safely be placed anywhere on the fixture. People often tend to underestimate the number of lighting fixtures needed in a home. In configuring the lighting plan for a house, it's useful to have a standard fixture for thematic use throughout. So we've developed our own fixture designs, intended to be accessible and affordable, with Remains Lighting, founded by David Calligeros, who reveres the craftmanship of fine metalwork. Designed and produced in the long-standing tradition of limited editions, these pieces have become semi-collectible.

1. Mirror and etched glass in this antique girandole in the living room provides a beautiful quality of light.

2, 3, 4. Hand-blown glass and plated brass fixtures are by Alan Wanzenberg for Remains Lighting.

5, 6. Glass hanging fixtures by Deborah Czeresko were commissioned through Site Specific Art Management, Inc.

7. Custom-made lantern was inspired by Arts & Crafts designer Karl Kipp.

8, 10. Table lamps were created with ceramicist Eric Bonnin for Remains Lighting.

9. Distressed Douglas fir lamp for Remains Lighting.

2

3

4

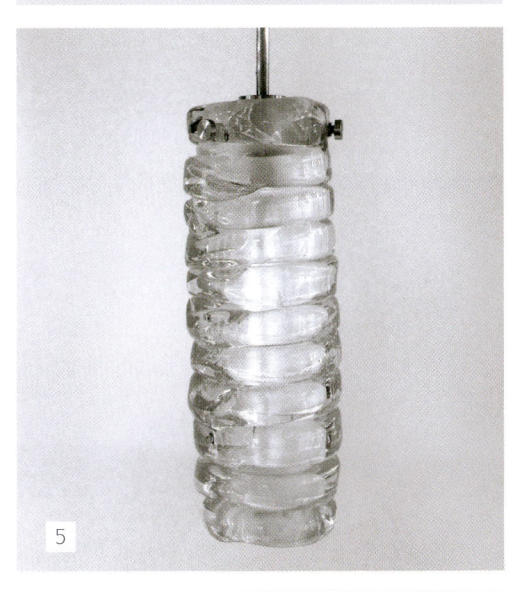
5

6

7

8

9

10

AN UPSTATE NEW YORK HOUSE BASED ON THE AMERICAN ARTS & CRAFTS MOVEMENT

The Robert Blacker house in Pasadena, California, designed by Greene & Greene, around 1908.

There has been an enduring bond of friendship between these clients, Jed, and myself. The diverse ethics and products of the English and American Arts & Crafts movement was a passionate interest we shared deeply. Traveling together, we visited many of the iconic structures in England and the United States. A highlight was seeing Taliesin East on a clear October day devoid of people, and with a guide who had lived on the property since her childhood. She was a fount of intimate and often hilarious Frank Lloyd Wright anecdotes. My friends had gone through the usual progression of looking for a second home. First in the Hamptons, then Bucks County, and finally Upstate New York. In the Hamptons, land of any scale was expensive and often not on the water. Bucks County had horrible zoning regulations. And finally Upstate, an more, the house would have no foreground to provide scale and intimacy. The house demonstrates a deep knowledge of the nature of the Arts & Crafts movement and comfortably maintains the different sensibilities from that era. It developed a vernacular sensibility that seems inevitably tied to the character of the region. We assembled an elite group of woodworkers, masons, textile artists, and metal fabricators to realize the complex design, and we worked hard to use local materials. The house is small by contemporary standards. It has a great intimacy and dimension. Each room is different, with the kitchen being perhaps the most complex, given its central position in the life of the house. In completing the interiors of the house, I used my familiarity with post-World War II French and American furniture. I saw the pieces as would have gone out of the house. That was a lesson I learned from Jed. Don't do the expected. Be contrary. The mix of furnishings spiced up the house and added great sophistication.

The base of the house is wrapped in locally harvested blue stone.

The house developed a vernacular sensibility that seems inevitably tied to the character of the region. We assembled an elite group of woodworkers, masons, textile artists, and metal fabricators to realize the complex design and worked hard to use local materials.

existing home with any historic interest was usually close to the road. In a newer home, one had to buy someone else's taste and remodeling. One night, at dinner, I suggested that they build their own. I did not suggest this out of self-interest, but because I felt they were the perfect couple to take on this task. Not only were they knowledgeable, but more important, they had the time and interest to make the project truly great. A few months passed before I got the call announcing they had bought land. During my first visit, we walked for about 20 minutes, and I remarked how exceptional the property was. They laughed and said we'd only seen about two of the 500 acres they had purchased. Most of the land was heavily forested and inaccessible. We settled quickly on a site for the house in an open meadow that took advantage of the extensive views, looking from east to west at the major mountain ranges of the Berkshires and Catskills. But there is a time-honored tradition to not locate a house on the top of the hill, as it would become too prominent in the landscape. Further-

The front hall in the Charnley-Persky House in Chicago, by Louis Sullivan and Frank Lloyd Wright, 1891.

a counterpoint to the Arts & Crafts movement that had been so dominant in the way we thought about the architecture. As a result, there is a mix. In the living room, pieces by George Nakashima are combined with wonderful chairs that are reminiscent of Gerald Summer, and are further combined with a sofa from B&B Italia, and a coffee table with a Lava-stone top and base of my design. Elsewhere, there are 1950s French chaises and lighting, and vintage William Haines chairs that create an unexpected combination. If it had all been done in the Arts & Crafts style, the impulse and spontaneity

The overhang over the porch door creates a play of light and shadow.

KITCHENS

In most homes, the kitchen is the center of all family activities. As its functions have become far more extensive, there is a great demand for it to look beautiful while also being highly functional. Often other rooms open up onto it, such as the mudroom, a dining area, or the family room. In many situations, I will introduce a natural wood into the kitchen. I find a natural wood provides warmth and is more forgiving and easier to maintain than painted surfaces. Painted surfaces, however, often work better with a variety of appliances. Tile is a favorite, especially when color is called for. And, even when using white tile, I appreciate the subtle variations in the tones, preferring things that are clean, and hygienic, but not too functional. The kitchen should provide a sense of well-being in a room where so much time is spent.

1. Aniline dyed cabinets with steel accents.

2. Flat panel-painted millwork, and marble counters.

3. Oak cabinets with tiles from Heath Ceramics.

4. Maple cabinets with a traditional Arts & Crafts profile.

5. Naturally finished wood cabinets with stainless steel appliances.

6. Open-front painted cabinets with a Pyrolave backsplash and stainless steel appliances.

7. Glass-fronted painted cabinets with maple butcher block counters.

8. Curved wood painted cabinetry for a sophisticated farmhouse look.

ART DECO TREASURES IN A PRISTINE MANHATTAN APARTMENT

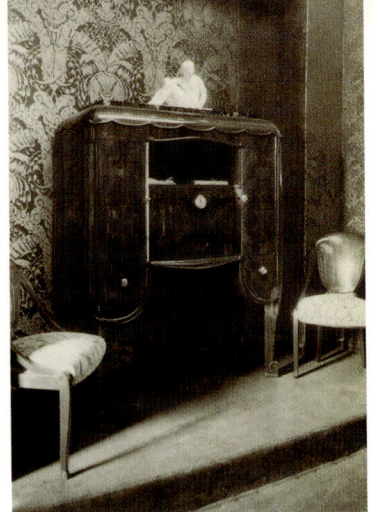

Superb Art Deco secretary is a 1923 Süe et Mare design.

For obvious reasons, after Jed died I was reluctant and circumspect about engaging in the areas of design that were in his scope of work and that might appear to challenge his unique sensibilities regarding decorative treatments, for instance, or his exceptional talent in building a collection for a client. However, by the late 1990s, I had made numerous trips to Paris, largely to assemble a wonderful collection of Art Deco furniture for a family in Sydney, Australia, where I had worked on a scholarly reconstruction of an old British Colonial home in the Eastern Suburbs. Experiencing the wily ways of Parisian antique dealers and the excitement of the hunt for beautiful and exceptional things made me want to do more work. I was beginning to learn that I liked decorating and, more important, that I was good at it! Around that time, I received a commission from a wonderful and intellectual Manhattan couple who had lived at the Beresford for the past decade in an apartment they had remodeled in the 1980s. Architecturally, they had taken apart the apartment and created an open floor plan that made it extremely contemporary, and gave it a recognizable, though dated, eighties look. The couple was restless and curious, wanting to reconstruct and begin to assemble a thorough and important collection of French Art Deco furnishings. They were familiar with the influential apartment Jed and I had created in the early 1990s for Maureen and Marshall Cogan. We researched the original layouts of the apartment. With regard to the decor, nothing had really been decided except for three key signature pieces: a screen by Jean Dunand, a marble and iron console by Edgar Brandt, and an exceptional secretary by Süe et Mare. These were "big-shouldered" and iconic pieces from the early part of the Art Deco period. When advising a client about starting a new area of collecting, I always advise them not to worry too much about the first things they buy, but rather to just go ahead and follow their hearts. That was the thinking with regard to these three pieces. The apartment was reconstructed to be similar to its original layout. Formality returned, and rooms were planned with the specific intent of housing their evolving collection. But significantly, new and far more luxurious materials—satinwood, parchment, afromosia floors, and white statuary marble—were introduced into this design scheme. As in the past, my challenge was to take a relatively small handful of edited materials and rework them expertly into a highly refined interior. As evidenced by earlier work, each material is subordinated to an overall composition that reflects refinement, hierarchy, and great restraint in their use. As we began to collect various pieces of furniture from the period, I looked a lot at French designer Jean-Michel Frank's wonderful and highly influential interiors. I also made a point of considering other designers. One in particular was Paul Depré-Lafon. For me, he had taken many of the iconic luxury materials and modernized them with a subtle reduction in their application. The early key pieces included a suite of chairs by Emile-Jacques Ruhlmann, a wonderful pair of Jean Royère chairs—bought from the great Parisian dealer Jacques Lacoste—and a beautiful rug by Marian Dorn from V'Soske. Collecting for me has always been about having confidence in what one acquires and how one displays it. We once assembled, at another client's request, a collection of beer bottles for the owner of Twin Farms. I believe you can take many things that might be disparate from each other and, with a show of confidence in the display, have the collection come across with remarkable impact. Subtleties also come into play. A beautifully vetted collection can be enhanced with one or two things that are totally anonymous, or from another era. A good example of this is the four Alexandre Noll chairs we purchased for the breakfast area in the apartment. Rare and exquisite, the chairs also point to a later era of design in that they date from post-World War II France. I encouraged using the unique designs in this everyday way, as it shows the clients' confidence in using the chairs as casual and everyday objects.

> As in the past, my challenge for this apartment was to take a relatively small handful of edited materials and rework them expertly into a highly refined interior.

Maison Jansen's luxurious 1937 bedroom for Helena Rubinstein had a gold satin bed in a quilted satin alcove.

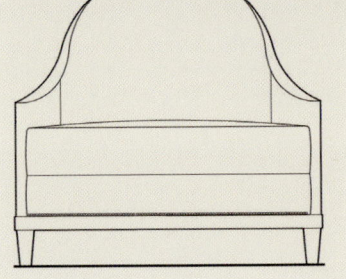

The graceful contour of classic French Art Deco furniture is reinterpreted in this sketch for a custom-made chair.

STAIRCASES

The staircase is where architects will often demonstrate their most skilled abilities. It is a design element that allows for great invention, and often many of the various aesthetic details that are in a home will culminate in its construction, summarizing the feeling of the house. A staircase can be heavily rendered and create a tour-de-force impact in its rigor, or it can be minimal and simplified in its design, contrasting with perhaps other, more detailed areas of the house. It is also an element in a home where one gets an opportunity to utilize various materials, starting with the flooring, but then often employing bronze or iron in the balustrade and handrail. I often engage with specific craftsmen, knowing that their unique talents will be showcased in the construction of the staircase.

1. Farmhouse staircase is authentic and simple, with its painted handrail and oak spindles.

2. Curved bronze handrail with curlicued spindles for a New York penthouse.

3. Hand-carved Cypress handrail was inspired by Mashrabiya screens.

4. Lacquered and patinated steel ribbons for a railing in a New York apartment.

5. Dog-legged staircase with interlocking and carved pine detailing.

6. Silhouetted and painted rhythmic balustrade for an Arts & Crafts house.

7. Stained cedar and steel supports for a staircase in a contemporary house.

2

3

4

5

6

7

VIBRANT COLORS AND BOLD PATTERNS FOR A NEW YORK FAMILY APARTMENT

A highway billboard poster was the focal point of this early 1970s interior.

I enjoy navigating between different historical periods and design styles. I cannot tell you how this happened, but I like it. There is great pleasure when you can resolve competing influences into a unified whole. I find so much contemporary design reductive and limited in the aesthetic challenges it takes on. In this commission, the client was familiar with the sophisticated and playful work I had done with Jed at Twin Farms. During our early discussions, we intentionally opted for an eclectic mix. From the time they had spent in Japan, they had not only absorbed the country's traditions, especially with regard to craftsmanship, but also the contrasting

Central Park. To unify the space, I used a stained walnut for the floors, which travels throughout the whole apartment and provides a consistency that holds the various diverse elements together. The art enhances the feeling of the project and fits well into the eclectic mood. Included are some beautiful, serene examples of Japanese calligraphy. It's a great pleasure to have the opportunity to work with artists and craftspeople for custom commissions, and on this project I was able to include several. In the dining area, I used the serious and animated lighting fixtures by the American artist Jeff Zimmerman. These pieces take the big, often static, oval dining table and

A beautiful tattoo by artist Ed Hardy inspired the tilework in the bathroom.

The big moves in this apartment included opening up the kitchen and family room to New York's Central Park, and giving structure and vibrancy to the bedrooms.

styles that are integrated in popular and commercial sensibilities. The program included combining two apartments at the Majestic building on New York's Upper West Side. The big moves were opening up the kitchen and family room toward Central Park, and giving structure and vibrancy to the bedrooms. Early on, we committed to dramatic color schemes for the daughters' bedrooms. The son's room was to be equally intense. I designed extensive built-ins and chose strong, deep blues and greens. An internal room, to function as a hangout room for the kids and to be shared by all the bedrooms, was to be big enough for a banquette and a large television. With the lack of any daylight, it was the right spot to employ a riotous mix of pattern and color. In response to this, I employed a subtle palette of color for the living room. By using bronze and silver, I worked off the hot cues from the back of the apartment, but toned them down. When using color this way, it's important to introduce pattern in order to create interest in the design. Examples of this are the interplay of the Christian Kreckles coffee table with the print on the fabric of the chairs, and the amorphous organic motif of the custom-made Edward Fields rug. The family room and the kitchen are in strong primary colors that contrast with the tree line of

The 1966 Eden fabric is a lively, colorful pattern by Alexander Girard.

give it a remarkable dynamic. Deborah Czeresko, with whom I have collaborated over the past couple of decades, created the lighting in the kitchen. We were also able to take a motif from a tattoo by Southern California artist Ed Hardy and really go to town with it in the bathroom shared by the two teenage daughters. The design, outrageous and fun, was executed by David Meitus, an old friend and client, in his Studium workshops.

Italian designer Osvaldo Borsani's 1950s chair was considered technologically advanced.

MATERIALS

Many years ago, Tom Whalen, a trusted adviser, who has often had a strong hand in the creation of our beautiful wood finishes for our numerous commissions, instructed me to always choose a wood for its original character. One shouldn't choose a wood and then try to distort it by bleaching it or use other techniques that severely alter its natural character. In that way, it's sort of like dating, as you need to like the person the way they are, not how you want them to be. The same philosophy applies to other materials, such as metal. Once you go through the detailed process of choosing a material, much of the hard work is done. Now the effort goes into creating the successful design that reveals the inherent beauty of the material that has been chosen.

1. Figured anigre wood has been used for the dining room's pocket door.

2. Pale celadon, aniline-dyed, quartered white oak in a paneled niche.

3. Stained pine boarding with cut-outs for the railing in a sleeping alcove.

4. Intense cobalt blue stained white ash lines a powder room at Twin Farms.

5. Pearwood with metal inlays on a Harmon hinged door, off a library in a New York apartment.

6. Stained pearwood acts as a background in a niche.

7. Satinwood covers the walls in a New York library.

8. Simple cedar has been stained for the walls in a beach house.

9. A mudroom in Vermont has built-in pine cabinetry.

10. In New York, Madrone wood boards have carved vertical detailing.

The interior was gutted, but the 1912 facade of the nineteenth-century townhouses remained.

A MAJOR RENOVATION FOR AN URBANE NEW YORK TOWNHOUSE

In the late 1970s and early 1980s, I would often visit the Frank Lloyd Wright home and studio in Oak Park, Illinois. Built and subsequently modified by him over the formative early years of his career, it was an exciting laboratory for his innovative work in residential design. The National Trust had acquired the property and had begun a painstaking analysis of the remarkable changes made over a 20-year period. It was fascinating to see the restless and often highly inventive mind of the great architect at work. After a long review, the question arose as to what date the house should be restored to, knowing that the choice of an exact date would eliminate the opportunity to see some of Wright's unique work. Eventually the year 1910 was decided on. It was the year Wright left his family and marriage for an entirely new chapter of his storied life. When one restores a house, there is always the assumption that one will modernize the building systems and improve the operations, but inevitably there are intangibles that must be evaluated in the maintenance and extension of the life of the structure. A few years ago, I was approached by a family to restore a townhouse on the Upper East Side of Manhattan. It was in poor shape, having been the Benin mission to the United Nations. My first visit was quite an experience, as the mission was still active and chaos reigned! The only things missing were live chickens and goats. It was quickly understood that the house would be totally rebuilt. The upper stories of the facade were a standard-issue brownstone from the late 1800s. However, a neoclassical addition had been put on the lower two stories around 1912 by the American architect Donn Barber. As we began studying and having lengthy discussions with the Landmarks Commission, it became clear that maintaining the facade was important. It showed the changes not only to the building and its esthetic sensibilities, but also to the canvas of New York over the successive decades. Maintaining this juxtaposition had value. In my work, I have seen both approaches work. Once we began developing the interiors, it was clear we needed one tour-de-force element that would unify the house. The staircase became that element. Continuous throughout all five stories, it is striking and dramatic, terminating at the top with a large skylight. In contrast, I chose to do very subtle architectural detailing. I knew the client had an impressive and eclectic art collection, and that my work needed to be subordinated to it. The spacious high-ceilinged second floor living room is home to works by such artists as Louise Nevelson, Sarah Morris, and Georg Baselitz. On the floor above, in the library, I decided against using traditional wall-paneling, as its appropriate dimensions might limit the size of the art to be displayed. On the top floor, I created a continuous wall of glazing reminiscent of a painter's atelier. As in all my work, I chose a narrow range of exquisite materials—walnut floors, mahogany doors and cabinetry, statuary white marble, and anigre wood for the kitchen.

The dramatic stair begins in the rebuilt entrance foyer.

> Once we began developing the interiors, it was clear we needed one tour-de-force element that would unify the house. The staircase became that element. Continuous throughout all five stories, it is striking and dramatic, terminating at the top with a large skylight.

Architect Samuel Marx's 1930s spiral staircase for a Chicago estate.

A room at the top of the house is reminiscent of a painter's atelier.

FIREPLACES

Often the fireplace is the last architectural element to be designed or chosen for a home, yet it is often the most emblematic piece in the design, as it indicates the historical period or the overall feeling. When appropriate, the use of an antique mantelpiece can provide an immediate sense of history and interest. It also often contrasts with some of the more contemporary elements in the design. Sometimes, I will design the fireplace. When there are multiple fireplaces in the home, it is important that they vary in design while also complementing each other. A new fireplace will generally coordinate better with other aspects of the interiors, such as the artwork, the paneling, and the cabinetry, where a more historic mantel might be distracting or out of scale. I generally don't cluster furniture around the fireplace, unless the goal is to create formality. My preference is for casual groups of furniture, which create comfort and make the fireplace less of a focal point.

1. In the living room, a Regency green and white marble mantelpiece with a Christophe Côme fire screen.

2. Arts & Crafts fireplace with historic Fulper tile.

3. All-brick firebox and surround with painted period mantelpiece.

4. Slate and metal mantelpiece with collage by artist Donald Baechler.

5. Elegant white marble mantelpiece with decorative iron painted screen.

ASSEMBLAGES

All of the clients I work with are collectors. What they collect is ultimately somewhat irrelevant, as they all share inquisitive, curious minds that want to acquire things. This is my nature as well. I live with things and am constantly changing and rearranging them. Often I create an environment to display what I call assemblies. One can have a single object on the table in a room, or many objects together. A single object can be evocative, however, when things are grouped well, it's like a successful dinner party—they are all animated, conversant, and interested in each other. While they can work singly, they're often enhanced when in a group. A successful assembly requires balance and careful editing. That's when it is a visual delight.

1. Scandinavian ceramics are displayed in the niches of a teak cabinet by Danish architect Mogens Koch. The stepstool is by American craftsman Sam Maloof.

2. Objects of diverse materials are elegantly silhouetted against a pale gray wall.

3. Twentieth-century French ceramics and an Alexander Noll pitcher, far left, sit on a Gustav Stickley sideboard.

4. A bowl-like lamp by French ceramicist Jean Besnard sits next to an abstract piece by French potter Camille Virot. On the wall is a charming drawing by Massachusetts-based artist Don Carney, whose brushwork refers to the surface texture of the lamp.

5, 6. Artworks in the library and dining room have been grouped because of their similar content.

7. In the bedroom an Alexandre Noll sculpture is flanked by a ceramic piece by Peter Horne and a lamp by Georges Jouve.

A TROPICAL COMPOUND THAT REFERENCES THE OLD WORLD CHARM OF PALM BEACH

The 1922 Villa des Cygnes, in Palm Beach, Florida, is one of architect Addison Mizner's masterworks.

When I think about the residential architecture of the past century, I think that most of the truly innovative houses that have had lasting influence are actually small in scale—Le Corbusier's Villa Savoye, Mies van der Rohe's Farnsworth House, the house Robert Venturi designed for his mother, and Frank Gehry's home in Santa Monica, California. When I consider the Great Society architects of the past century, such as David Adler in Chicago and Addison Mizner in Palm Beach, they work at a larger scale, with a more complex social program for the home,

I never want my clients to feel highly self-conscious in their own homes. When I started to work on this house, it was for a client with whom I had done other projects. We had a familiar, respectful, and successful relationship.

and typically weave a historical vernacular design tradition into the work. Why? My assumption is that in modern architecture, concepts are often abstract and reductive, whereas in vernacular design, there are motifs and details that can be easily adapted and expanded, often generating out of traditional forms. When I started to work on this particular house in Florida, it was for a family with whom I had done several other projects. We had a familiar, respectful, and accomplished relationship, which always augurs well for the success of a project. From earlier work in my career, I understood that with a large building program I should draw, in this instance, from the rich architectural tradition of such Palm Beach architects as Addison Mizner. His houses have a wonderful domesticity and charm, but are solid as well. As I have done on similar projects, I broke down the building program into a discrete series of elements, a compound that allowed for a hierarchy of building types. The site for this home was a spectacular three-acre parcel of land on a rugged portion of the Atlantic Coast, only adding to my belief in the appropriateness for us to work in this vernacular style. The property consists of four structures—the main house, a guesthouse, a caretaker's house, and a garage. While I wanted all the major rooms of the main house to face toward the ocean, it was equally important to create alternate spaces. I never want my clients to feel highly self-conscious in their own homes. In this house, one enters from the north via a courtyard and sees very little of the compound. The courtyard creates intimacy, and reduces the mass and scale of the buildings. From our past experience, this clients' preference is to work with a narrow palette of materials for the design—tiled roofs, stucco walls, and mahogany windows. The terrace and stonework is coquina, a traditional and distressed coral stone. We used it judiciously in areas where it was going to provide maximum impact, such as to frame the modest front door, which contrasts with the luxurious, highly sophisticated interior. The entrance hall that opens onto the living room makes an immediate statement to visitors. One begins to see the confident mix of an Italian center table on a

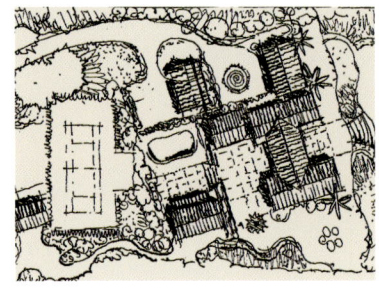

The site planning included the placement of a number of different buildings in the compound.

Making the property—both its facade, above, and front entrance, right—look and feel discreet was important.

Chinese rug, which is then complemented by a remarkable painting by the American artist Cy Twombly that has been hung at the end of the living room. It's a sensuousness that speaks to comfort. There are opulent but relaxed silks, linens, and cottons, and a color palette that deliberately rotates around a handful of colors in order to magnify what is really exceptional—the artworks themselves, such as pieces by Ellsworth Kelly, Louise Bourgeois, and Brice Marden.

CUSTOM DESIGN

My commissions always require some degree of custom design, usually in terms of furniture and often in hardware and lighting, as well as bedside tables and coffee tables of such unique materials as antique tiles, Pyrolave, and arcane stone. What drives the custom designs? Often it's the lack of availability of an appropriately sized piece specific to the proportions of the space. It's usually difficult to find a suitable dining table. A beautiful set of dining chairs can be found ready-made, and are rarely commissioned, as they are more challenging to make. In my selection of table and chairs, I like to contrast the two. Otherwise, if the table and the chairs are of a similar style, the atmosphere becomes static. The focus of the table's design is its top, because it distills the beauty of the piece's shape. Less consideration is given to the base, which can become lost once the chairs are brought in. The ability to make this furniture is an outcome of the exceptional craftspeople whose talents I have fostered over decades. My partner in manufacturing hardware is The Nanz Company, founded by Steve Nanz, who works with the company's co-owner, Carl Sorenson. Our work together has further developed their exceptional product line.

1. Small mahogany bedside table was custom-designed for the clients' son's bedroom.

2, 4, 10, 12. Custom-made upholstered pieces allow for clients' special requirements.

5, 6, 8. Small tables and a bench have been designed to be paired with larger-scaled pieces.

3, 7, 9, 11, 13. Dining tables are often custom-designed to complement sets of antique chairs.

AN APARTMENT DISTINGUISHED BY PARISIAN FURNISHINGS AND CONTEMPORARY ART

A Parisian dining room by Jean-Charles Moreux, early 1940s.

Often, clients tend to stick to a familiar and established path in their design choices, without realizing that there are alternatives that are close in sensibility but potentially more sophisticated and refined. A spacious apartment in original condition, located in the esteemed San Remo building on Manhattan's Upper West Side, had been acquired by my clients and needed to be completely reorganized to suit a more contemporary lifestyle. The whole space was gutted and rebuilt; everything was reconstructed and produced by my office. I could see from what the clients had already collected in their previous homes that

fireplace. This project gave me an early opportunity to purchase the work of Ado Chale, the late twentieth-century Belgian-born sculptor and furniture designer. The clients also acquired pieces by the French designer Pierre Jeanneret, which juxtapose simple construction with great, sophisticated proportions. There were also numerous pieces that were custom-made for the apartment—specifically two rugs—one for the family room by V'Soske, of my design; the other by F. J. Hakimian for the dining room that utilized a Japanese fan motif as its design inspiration and was made from antique kilim remnants.

Vintage wall sconce by Max Ingrand.

There existed a nascent sensibility that could be developed into something exceptional. Numerous pieces were custom-made for the apartment, specifically two rugs.

there existed a nascent sensibility that could be developed into something exceptional. We took a quick trip to Paris, where one of the first things we saw, and subsequently acquired, was a marvelous folding game table by André Sornay. The intricate and rational design for the table and its ability to expand and contract was a subtle and ingenious piece of engineering that we all admired. We were also attracted to the incredible tactility of the wood and the wonderful simplicity of its decorative use of nailheads. The scrubbed oak pine provided a perfect release from the rational organization of the apartment. It had a sensuousness that contrasted perfectly with the simple and reduced detailing of the interior architecture I had designed. This early purchase solidified many of our subsequent design choices, such as a beautiful sideboard in the dining room, a lacquer table that was a collaboration between Jean Dunand and Eugène Printz, and the sconces by Eugène Printz that flank the mirror by the

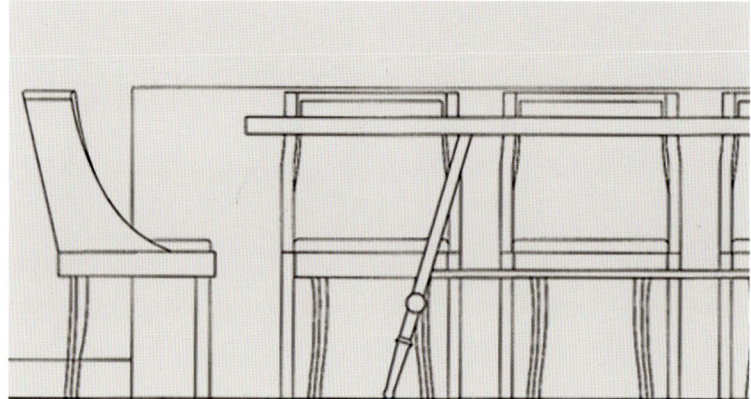

Sketch of formal dining room with a table for 10 people and its set of custom-made chairs.

Moderne chair by French designer Pierre Jeanneret was a new addition to the living room.

BATHROOMS

Perhaps nowhere else in the home is there a greater opportunity for sensuousness and a complex display of materials than in the bathroom. I have two approaches. One is a cool design that is abstract, often minimal, and very restrained. The other is hot, voluptuous, and with a great variety of materials. Both are emotional solutions, and both require great craftsmanship and a careful editing of details. A good example of using one material in a committed way is statuary white marble. The other approach often utilizes many diverse materials, combined in an elegant and well-crafted manner, allowing me to introduce a more historical approach, by bringing in paneling and historic tiles. Limited space is less important than a good layout. When successful, the bathroom is one of the areas of the home that can provide pleasure on a daily basis.

1. White marble with polished nickel and walnut cabinetry in the master bathroom.

2. Painted cabinets detailed with wrought-iron hardware.

3. White marble sink on satin-finished nickel legs in a Vermont house.

4. Soapstone and wood vanity with finger joints, and metal and wood hardware.

5. In New York, custom-made marble sinks with glass legs.

6. Duravit sink with custom metal detailing and wall-mounted plumbing fittings.

7. Ice Stone countertop is supported with an oak base.

8. Malibu tile wainscotting with a satin nickel basin and black marble countertop.

9. Custom-made wrought-iron base and glass counter.

10. White marble counter and patinated steel skirting.

A COUNTRY HOUSE INSPIRED BY THE SPIRIT OF CLASSICAL SHAKER ARCHITECTURE

The historic Shaker Meetinghouse in Sabbathday Lake, Maine, 1794.

I wanted to create a home that was clearly part of the vocabulary of the area, but was more astringent, tailored, refined, and crisp—like the air at the beach in the morning.

Why is a simple black cocktail dress so popular and enduring? Could it be that it allows the wearer to accessorize it, and that the personality of the wearer becomes more important than the simplicity of the dress itself? If one started with something more flamboyant, the effect would not be the same. We are often drawn to these wonderfully simple elements in our everyday life. In the Hamptons, there are streets outside the historic estate area that are intimate and familiar because of the accumulation of wonderful old cottages built over time, and which are so beautifully sited in the environment. Yet, the current trend is quite the opposite. While we are drawn to these marvelous and picturesque areas, due in part to the enormous value of the land, we tear down the structures and build significantly larger, often overwhelming, and potentially inappropriate structures for these unique settings. Having lived on the ocean in Water Island, New York, for several decades, I like the simplicity of beach life and the respite that it gives from everyday demands. The long periods of unstructured time offer one the opportunity to recharge oneself. The family that had approached me for this particular commission lived in a cottage on a street that exemplified these marvelous traits of simplicity and originality. Yet the property they acquired had two houses in severe disrepair—one prosaic and nondescript, the other charming but far gone. The property had once been owned by the trailblazing scientist Madame Curie's granddaughter, and had a quirkiness in its layout and materials that I truly admired. But saving the buildings was not possible. Thinking about the new house that we would be building, I immediately turned away from the notion of the classic Shingle Style. For me, that style had been degraded in many instances due to the aggressively inflated homes built in the flurry of construction of the last decade. I wanted to create a home that was clearly part of the vocabulary of the area, but more astringent, tailored, refined, and crisp—like the air and environment can be on a morning at the beach. So I looked at the early and reductive style of Shaker architecture from the nineteenth century. It was simple and clean, and thoroughly American. It was that neutral palette that would allow both a sense of personality in design and decorating to be revealed, while maintaining the contextual building traditions of this beautiful part of the Hamptons. I had worked with Susan Child, a landscape architect who was based in Boston in the past. She brought an elegant and familiar plan to the early stages of the project. Her input and desire to site the house closer to the street gave it an immediate history, making it appear more significant and connected the building to the traditions of the area. A tremendous effort was also made to maintain the large, decades-old trees that populated the site. In all of my work, a lot of attention is paid to proportion. The choice of windows is indicative of one of the Shaker characteristics I truly admire. There is a kind of repetition, but also a spontaneity as the windows are placed in locations relative to what is required for the interior rooms. The secondary buildings are built with wood shingles and have the identical, although reduced, proportions of the main house, and clearly reference the agricultural and storage barns in the area. In the kitchen, I chose Danby, Vermont marble, locally supplied bluestone, and reclaimed Cypress, which has a rich driftwood-like feeling, and was something that I specifically wanted to use because it had been in one of the original structures on the property. Color—primarily blue and some greens—was used thematically, in reference to color as used by the Shakers, but done in a sympathetic and quiet way, to draw out the inherent beauty in the wood.

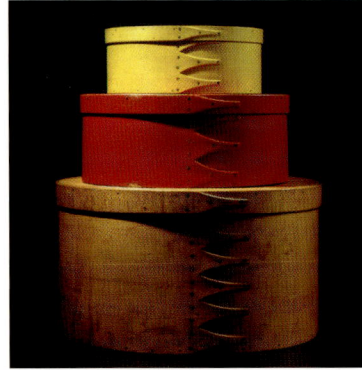

Colorful oval boxes are a Shaker classic.

Repetition and spontaneity define the placement of the windows.

The mudroom has Shaker-style pegs and paneled walls.

DOORWAYS

It would be nearly impossible to design a home without doors. They are not only fundamental to the language of a residence but are often very under-considered and not utilized to their fullest design capacity. Designing a great-looking door, one of the highlights of the interior design process, can be a challenging endeavor. Doors should not become overly complex, as that's when they become self-conscious. But they should not be extremely minimal either, so designing the right door is like seasoning a dish, the door being necessary to bring out the flavors of the other elements in the house. I generally utilize the traditional construction elements of a door—the vertical styles, the horizontal rails, and the center panel. They not only add beauty and proportion to the work, but demonstrate detail and craftsmanship. Texture, stain, and color can be added into the mix when one uses natural woods in an exceptional way.

1. The overscaled board-and-batten exterior door is in the guesthouse.

2. Natural stained-wood doors lead to a screened porch in a pool house.

3. Stained and distressed white oak-raised panel doors are dramatic in a New York apartment.

4. Teak pocket doors have stained glass panels in an Arts & Crafts interior.

5. Satinwood doors with dark wood inlays in a Manhattan dressing room.

6. In Florida, a raised panel mahogany door opens out from the entrance foyer.

7. A triangulated series of doors frame a view through a series of bedrooms in a Vermont house.

3
COMING HOME
...to the private places that provide me with renewal, rest, and uninhibited mental and emotional exploration.

BAY HOUSE, WATER ISLAND, NEW YORK

WATER ISLAND

In the summer of 1986, the Venturi house in Vail, Colorado, was sold. Work was demanding and preoccupying, so we gave little thought to acquiring another place away from New York. However, in the summer of 1987, during a memorable visit with friends to the Fire Island Pines, we had the notion to consider getting a place there, as the setting gave us the sense of a connection with nature similar to what we had had in Vail. The lifestyle was simple and the pleasures were basic—there was no shopping to speak of, no cars, and the social life was low-key. We decided to find a home on the Great South Bay so we could come and go at will on our own by boat, an experience which both Jed and I were comfortable with from our youth. Our search was brief. The first house we were shown was the Bay House that had been owned by the fashion designer Perry Ellis, who had died prematurely the previous year. Situated in Water Island, a remote community to the east of the Pines, the house was small, humble, and utterly unpretentious. On our initial visit, our dogs, Archie and Amos, were playing happily on the deck. Jed looked at me and said, "Well, the dogs love it, so I think we have to get it." Only 50 miles from the city, it was easily accessible and relaxing. Over the following years, we acquired the companion house on the Atlantic Ocean and created a number of designs for both structures. Twenty-five years later, the magic and uniqueness of the place still radiates for me. The Ocean House is an extrovert—hot, bright, and emotional—while the Bay House is an introvert—cool, dark, and quiet.

WEST 67TH STREET

I find the block between Central Park West and Columbus Avenue on West 67th Street in Manhattan to be one of the most architecturally significant in the city. On it are five buildings that date from the early 1900s, with large, double-story duplex living spaces or studios, the most famous of these being the Hotel des Artistes. The Hotel and its neighbor across the street reveal vertical windowed spaces on their street facades. The other three buildings, which share closely planned layouts done by their common architects, have their windows in the rear. Facing north, these are the more authentic. Artists of the building's era preferred northern light for its soft, non-directional quality, as well as its suitability for painting. I've always been intrigued more by the quality and variety of the spaces that these apartments provide. My home is in the Central Park Studios, and I am only the second occupant of the apartment. Having spent 32 years there—over half my life—without ever wishing to dismantle or erase its history and patina, the apartment has been a constant laboratory for ideas about furniture, lighting, and collecting. I see my home as a chance to do small, incremental studies that are early ideas for potentially larger constructions of something similar, usually for clients. As confident as I want to feel about the work that I do professionally, I see these efforts in my home as experimental. I continue these explorations as part of a larger process of growth and knowledge.

TAGHKANIC

In the fall of 2001, I began looking at property to the north of New York. With no specific intent to build right away, and for no reason related to the recent tragedy, I was restless, thinking about the decade ahead. Fifty years old and with 20 years of work behind me, I knew that I was at a midpoint in many ways—professionally, emotionally, and physically. I wanted a long-term project into which I could dream myself away. Speaking with friends, I was directed to a property that was for sale but not yet on the market. Close to the Taconic Parkway and just over 100 miles from the city, the land was comprised of a long, descending ravine that bisected two large parcels of fields contained in a now-defunct dairy farm. On the land was an internal creek that traversed open meadows, wetlands, and mature stands of hemlock, oak, and beech with large rock formations and stepped waterfalls. My good friend Mark McDonald, who has lived in the area for decades, remarked on its uniqueness, given the combination of rugged features and its proximity to the city. I bought the property and became at once engaged in all the details and overwhelmed by what to do. Peter Kelly, a talented and pragmatic landscape architect with tremendous experience, guided me in ways that were immediately helpful and profoundly beneficial. Peter advised me to take my time in studying the land and recommended that I contact a company called Shelter-Kit, located in New Hampshire, which makes small dwellings for remote sites. Built of pre-cut individual pieces from quality materials, the structures are not only stylish but rather simple, practical, and reasonable to acquire. Implicit in Peter's suggestion was that we would have an oasis to hang out in after we began hiking the land, where we would make notes about the existing vegetation and topographic details. Ultimately, I built three small cabins that we use throughout the year as our lodging and as a respite from our active lives in New York. Unit One is reserved for sleeping, and the largest one is where we make meals and hang out during the day. The smallest of the three contains a bathroom and storage. The setting recalls many emotions that I experience when on Water Island, Vail, and from my early life.

The setting gave us the sense of a connection with nature similar to what we had had in Vail.

1. View of the Bay House from the dock.

2. Summer sunset over the bay.

3. The Ocean House as seen from the dunes.

4. The paneled library and dining area in the Bay House.

5. Aerial view of Water Island with the Bay House, left, and the Ocean House.

6. The living room area in the Bay House.

OCEAN HOUSE, WATER ISLAND, NEW YORK

> The apartment has been a constant laboratory for ideas about furniture, lighting, and collecting.

1. One of the Gothic-style buildings, on West 67th Street, that date from 1918.

2. Photographed in 2010, the double-story living room is shown as it was furnished at the time.

3. The bathroom, with its antique Porcher bathtub and Pewabic Studios tile.

4. In the bedroom, a headboard by George Nakashima, a side table by François Jouve, and an early lamp by Dirk van Erp.

5. Ernie naps in the upstairs hallway.

6. Displayed on the mantelpiece, pieces of pottery from the village of La Borne, France.

WEST 67TH STREET,
NEW YORK, NEW YORK

I wanted a long-term project into which I could dream myself away.

1. Wooden walkways lead to the cabins.

2. The view to the west is of the Catskill Mountains.

3. Exterior and deck of the Main Cabin.

4. Prints by artist Frank Moore in the open living space of the Main Cabin.

5. A winding trail leads to the waterfall.

6. The kitchen in the Main Cabin is simple and functional.

7. The metal bench by Jim Rose at the Upper Cabin.

UPSTATE NEW YORK

INDEX

Adler, David, 27, 162
Alexander, Christopher, 17
Allen, Barbara, 7
Ammann, Thomas, 7, 25
Anderson, Ross, 19
Andrews, John, 18
Architects Collaborative (Cambridge, MA), 21
Art Deco style, 26, 35, 66
Arts & Crafts design, 7, 26, 54, 56, 64, 102, 156, 220
Ashkar, Tarek, 22
assemblages, 160
Australia, 35

B&B Italia, 57
Baechler, Donald, 136
Barber, Donn, 27, 122
bathrooms, 194
Baugh, Keith, 30
Beauvais Carpets, 90
Benson, W.A.S., 54
Berkeley (CA), 16, 17, 21
Berry, Kitty McGraw, 18
Bertoia, Harry, 138
Besnard, Jean, 160
Bonnin, Eric, 54
Booth, Nagle & Hartray, 22
Borsani, Osvaldo, 104
Boston City Hall, 20
Bourgeois, Louise, 162
Boynton, Florence Treadwell, 17–18
Brandt, Edgar, 66
Brant, Peter, 27
Brant, Sandra, 27, 28
Brown, Carter, 12, 14
Burg, Linda, 27

cabinets, 7, 64, 194
California: Berkeley, 16, 17, 21; Los Angeles, 16; San Francisco, 18; Sonoma County, 18
Calligeros, David, 54
Carney, Don, 160
carpets and rugs, 90
Cassandre, A.M., 38
Castle Park (MI), 12, 14
Central Park Studios, 225
ceramics collections, 160
Chafe, Ado, 184
Chapas Textiles, 90
Chareau, Pierre, 38
Charnley-Persky House, 56
Child, Susan, 92, 196
China Trade School, 38
Clonsilla, 27
Cobb, Henry, 24
Cogan, Maureen and Marshall, 31, 33, 66
Colacello, Bob, 7, 25
collaboration, 138
collections, 160

Colorado, 28–30, 225
Côme, Christophe, 136
commission work, 182
Connecticut, 22, 27–28, 31, 92
Converse, Edmund, 27
Conyers Farm, 27–28, 31, 32
Cotton House, 27
countertops, 64, 194
custom design work, 182
custom hardware, 182
Cyjar, Keith, 31
Czeresko, Deborah, 54, 104

Dalton, John, 24
Davis, Angela, 16
de Menil, Dominique, 26
Dean, Tommy, 7
Depré-Lafon, Paul, 66
Design Research, 21
DeWoody, Beth Rudin, 6–7
DeWoody, James, 7
dining rooms, 66, 182, 184
doors and doorways, 220
Dorn, Marion, 66
Duncan, Isadora, 17–18
Durand, Jean, 66, 184

Eisenman, Peter, 20
England, 7
Erp, Dirk van, 225
Esherick, Joseph, 17, 18
Esherick, Wharton, 138
Evanston, IL, 10, 11, 16
exotic woods, 38

fabric pattern and texture, 90
Fairchild, John, 7
Faneuil Hall Marketplace, 21
Fields, Edward, 104
fireplaces, 136. See also mantelpieces
First Church of Christ, Scientist (Berkeley, CA), 21
Fisher, Walter and family, 22
Florida, 162
France, 21, 26, 34, 66
Frank, Jean-Michel, 38, 66
Frank, Josef, 138
Freed, James, 25
Fulper tile, 136

Gehry, Frank, 162
Genet, Jean, 16
Gibbs, Christopher, 27
Girard, Alexander, 104
Glass House, the, 22, 24
Graves, Michael, 20
Greene and Greene, 56
Grenadines, 27
Gropius, Walter, 18, 20, 21
Gropius House, 18, 20
Guinness, Catherine, 25
Gwathmey, Charles, 20

Hadley, Albert, 28, 38
Haines, William, 57
Hakimian, F.J., 90, 184
Hakimian, Doriyn, 17
the Hamptons, 7, 56, 196
Hardy, Ed, 104
Harvard Graduate School of Design, 18, 20
Heath Ceramics, 64
Helduk, John, 20
Hotel des Artistes, 225
Housing Works, 31
Howe, George, 27
Hughes, Fred, 7, 25, 26, 34
Hurricane Island (ME), 15

I.M. Pei & Partners, 24
Idaho, 35
Illinois, 10, 11, 16, 22
Immeuble Clarté, 21
India, 30
Ingrand, Max, 184
Italy, 21–22

Jackson, J. B., 17
Jagger, Bianca, 7
Jagger, Mick, 26–27
Japan, 7
Java, 7
Javits Convention Center (New York), 25
Jeanneret, Pierre, 184
Jim Thompson House, 7
John F. Kennedy Presidential Library and Museum, 24
Johnson, Jed, 6, 7, 25–34
Johnson, Philip, 22, 24
Jones, Katie, 26
Jouve, François, 225
Jouve, Georges, 160
Juhl, Finn, 138

Kallmann, Gerhard, 20–21
Kallmann, McKinnell and Knowles, 21
Katz, Alex and Ida, 7
Kelly, Ellsworth, 162
Kelly, Peter, 7, 225
Ketchum (ID), 35
King, Charles, 31
Kinnicutt, Dorothy May, 28
Kipp, Karl, 7
kitchens, 64
Koch, Mogens, 160
Kreckles, Christian, 104
Krier Brothers, 20
Kwiatkowski, Henryk de, 28

Lacoste, Jacques, 66
lacquer table, 184
Landscapes (Jackson), 17
Le Corbusier, 21–22, 162
Lescaze, William, 34–35
lighting, 38, 54
Lindeberg, Harrie T., 27, 28
Lord Glenconner, 27
Los Angeles (CA), 16
Lyndon, Donlyn, 17

Måås-Fletterström, Märta, 138
Maloof, Sam, 138
Maine, 7, 15, 138, 196
mantelpieces, 6, 7, 38. See also fireplaces
Marden, Brice, 162
Mare, Süe et, 66
Marx, Samuel, 122
Maybeck, Bernard, 17, 21
McDonald, Mark, 225
Meier, Richard, 20
Meigs, Arthur I., 27
Messel, Oliver, 27
Metras, David, 104
Meyer, Averil, 7
Michigan, 7, 14
Miller, Jane, 26
Mizner, Addison, 162
Moderne chair, 184
Monacin, Susan, 19
Monroe, A. Randolph, 17
Montgomery, Roger, 17
Moore, Charles, 17, 18
Moore, Frank, 234
Moreux, Jean-Charles, 184
Mustique Island (Grenadines), 27

Nakashima, George, 57
Nakashima, Mira, 138, 225
Nanz, Steve, 182
The Nanz Company, 182
New York; Hamptons, 7, 56, 196; Manhattan, 26–27, 30, 31, 34–35, 66
Noll, Alexandre, 66, 160
Norman, Dorothy, 34, 35
Norman townhouse, 34–35
Norman, Edward, 34
Notre Dame du Haut chapel, 21
Nutting, Wallace, 92

Old Hickory Furniture, 14, 15
Outward Bound, 15–16

Palace Hotel, 16
Palm Beach (FL), 162
Paris, 34, 66
Parker, MacRae, 34
Parish-Hadley Associates, 28
Parr Family, 12
Parson Capen House, 92
A Pattern Language: Towns, Buildings, Construction (Alexander), 17
Persky, Lester, 7
Pewabic Studios, 6, 7, 225
Phillips Exeter Academy, 235
pilgrimages, 21–24, 24–25
Poet sofa, 138
Porcher bathtub, 225
Portland Museum of Fine Arts, 24
Printz, Eugène, 184

Quincy Market, 21

Remains Lighting, 54
restaurant, Joe Allen, 18
Rittel, Horst, 17
Robert Blacker House, 56
Robert Venturi House, 28, 30
Robertson, Mary, 10, 28
Rose, Jim, 234
Rosentiel, Lewis, 27
The Rouse Company, 21
Rowe, Colin, 20
Royère, Jean, 35, 66
Rubinstein, Helena, 66
rugs and carpets, 90, 184
Ruhlmann, Emile-Jacques, 66
Ryoanji, 138

Salto, Axel, 138
Samuels, John, Jr., 7
San Francisco (CA), 16
San Remo building, 184
Sayer, Eric, 31
Schlumberger, Christiane, 26
Schwartz, Frederic, 19
Schwarz, Michael, 12
sconces, 38
Sea Ranch, 17, 18
26–27, 30, 31, 34–35, 66
56, 196; Manhattan,
New York; Hamptons, 7,
Shaker Meetinghouse, 196
Shelter-Kit, 225
sideboard, 184
Sister Parish, 28
Site Specific Art Management, Inc., 54
Skowhegan, 7
Smith, Thurston Twigg, 31
Sonoma County (CA)
Sorensen, Carl, 182
Sornay, André, 184
St. Andrews University, 20
staircases, 22, 102, 122
Stargroves, 26, 27
Stern, Robert A.M., 20, 24
Stickley, Gustav, 54, 160
Stirling, James, 20
Studium, 104
Süe et Mare, 66
Sullivan, Louis, 56
Summer, Gerald, 57
Switzerland, 21
Sydney, 35
Sydney, Australia, home, 35, 66

Tagkhanic (NY), 225, 234, 235
Temple of Wings, 17
Tennant, Colin, 27
textiles, 90
Thailand, 7
Thompson, Ben, 21
Thompson, David G., 138
Thompson, Jim, 7
Thompson, Robert Thorne Miniature Rooms, 10, 27
tropical woods, 38
Turnbull, William, Jr., 17, 18
Twin Farms, 14, 31, 34, 66, 120
Twombly, Cy, 162

utopian houses, 22, 24, 138

Vail, Colorado, 28–30, 225
van der Rohe, Mies, 162
Venturi, Robert, 28, 30, 162
Vermont, 14, 31, 66
Villa des Cygnes, 162
Villa Fallet, 21
Virot, Camille, 160
Visual Squalor and Social Disorder (Thompson), 21
V'Soske, 66, 90, 184

Walter Fisher House, 22
Wanzenberg, Doris and Henry, 15
Warhol, Andy, 7, 24, 25–26, 34
Water Island (NY), 196, 224, 226, 227
Wax, Ruby, 18
Webster, Stephen, 25, 26
Wegner, Hans, 138
West 67th Street (NY), 225, 230, 231
Whalen, Tom, 120
Whitaker, Richard, 17
Whitney, David, 24
Windsor chair, 92
Winslow Homer Studio, 7
wood types, 120
Wright, Frank Lloyd, 56, 122

YMCA, 12

Zimmerman, Jeff, 104

CREDITS

Every effort has been made to locate the individual holders of copyrights. Any omissions will be corrected in future printings.

WILLIAM ABRANOWICZ: Back cover; opposite half title: pages 39-54; page 56, stone detail, porch door; pages 57-64; pages 67-90; page 91, detail number 6; pages 93-102; pages 105-120; page 121, number 6: pages 123-136; page 138; page 122, top right; bottom right: pages 139-160; page 162, center right; bottom right: pages 163-182; page 184, top right; bottom right: pages 185-194; page 195, number 5; page 196, center right, bottom right; pages 197-220; page 221, number 5; page 230, numbers 1, 2, 3, 5; page 234, numbers 1, 3, 4, 5, 6, 7; pages 235-237; page 241.

DON FREEMAN: Page 28, center left; page 31, top right: page 65, number 1; page 121, numbers 1, 7; page 161, numbers 3, 6; page 195, numbers 4, 9; page 221, number 4; page 226, numbers 4, 6.

JOHN M. HALL: Page 26, center left, bottom left; page 27, center right, bottom right; page 28, center left; page 29; page 31, center right, bottom right; pages 32-33; page 34, top left; page 65, numbers 3, 6; page 103, numbers 4, 6; page 121, number 3; page 195, numbers 1, 3, 7; page 224.

MICHELLE ROSE: Page 6, numbers 1, 3, 6; page 12, top left; page 22, top left, center left; page 55, number 5; page 65, numbers 2, 4, 5, 7; page 91, center right, bottom right; page 103, numbers 1, 2, 3, 5; numbers 2, 3, 4, 5; page 103, numbers 1, 2, 3, 5; page 121, numbers 2, 4, 5, 8, 9; page 122, top left; bottom right; page 137, numbers 1-4; page 161, numbers 1, 2, 4, 5; page 195, numbers 2, 6, 8; page 221, numbers 1, 2, 3, 6; page 230, numbers 4, 6; page 231; pages 232-233.

Cover: Collage, 1971, by Alan Wanzenberg, photographed by Christopher Burke Studios. Page 6, numbers 2, 4, 5: Personal Collection of Alan Wanzenberg. Page 10, from top: Personal Collection of Alan Wanzenberg; Courtesy of the Evanston History Center: Mrs. James Ward Thorne, A11. Rhode Island Parlor, 1820, c. 1940, Miniature room, mixed media, Interior: 10 1/8 x 18 1/4 x 17 1/2 inches, Gift of Mrs. James Ward Thorne, 1942.491. Photography © The Art Institute of Chicago: Mrs. James Ward Thorne, A31: Tennessee Entrance Hall, 1835, c. 1940, Miniature room, mixed media, Interior: 14 1/8 x 14 1/2 x 30 1/4 inches, Gift of Mrs. James Ward Thorne, 1942.511, Photography © The Art Institute of Chicago. Page 11: Personal Collection of Alan Wanzenberg. Page 12, center left: Public domain; bottom left: Personal collection of Alan Wanzenberg. Page 13: Personal collection of Alan Wanzenberg. Page 14: Castle Park Meeting House, from Castle Park 1896-1973. Page 15, from top: cherrygallery.com; personal collection of Alan Wanzenberg; public domain: courtesy of the Hurricane Island Foundation. Page 16, from top: Personal collection of Alan Wanzenberg; public domain: personal collection of Alan Wanzenberg. Page 17, top right: © Jim Alinder, Bettmann/CORBIS. Page 18, bottom right: Berkeley Architectural Heritage Association/Dimitri Shipounoff Collection. Page 18, from top: Courtesy of EHDD; photograph by Shanna Ravindra; personal collection of Alan Wanzenberg; public domain. Page 19: Personal collection of Alan Wanzenberg, Page 20, from top: © Wayne Andrews/Esto/All rights reserved; Courtesy of Historic New England; photograph by Barry Denwitt, Courtesy of MIMOA; Ezra Stoller © Esto. All rights reserved. Page 21, from top: Public domain: Library of Congress, Prints & Photographs Division; HABS; photograph by Daniella Thompson; personal collection of Alan Wanzenberg. Page 22, top left: From Modern Interiors; bottom left: Personal collection of Alan Wanzenberg. Page 23: Personal collection of Alan Wanzenberg. Page 24, from top: Photograph by David McCabe; personal collection of Alan Wanzenberg; Robert Knudsen, White House/John F. Kennedy Presidential Library and Museum; Craig M. Becker. Page 25, top right: Photograph by Brian Dubé. Page 26, top left: Personal collection of Alan Wanzenberg. Page 27, top right: Personal collection of Alan Wanzenberg. Page 28, top left: From Domestic Architecture of H.T. Lindeberg, 1940 (Acanthus Press, 2003 edition); bottom left: Personal collection of Alan Wanzenberg. Page 30, top left, center left: Personal collection of Alan Wanzenberg; bottom left: Photograph by Keith Baugh, from Early New York Subway Graffiti 1973-1975 by Keith Baugh. Page 34, from second from top: Personal collection of Alan Wanzenberg; Patrick McMullan; Chris Dunn. Page 35, top right: Scott Frances, bottom right: Personal collection of Alan Wanzenberg. Page 38, clockwise: Courtesy of www.internationalposter.com, Boston MA, from Pierre Chareau; Courtesy of Skinner, www.skinnerinc.com. Page 55, numbers 1, 2, 3, 7, 8, 9: Remains Lighting, number 5: Peter Kolk; number 6: Personal collection of Alan Wanzenberg. Page 56 top left: This item is reproduced by permission of the Huntington Library, San Marino, CA; center right: Photo copyright by James Caulfield/All rights reserved. Page 66.

clockwise: Archives Mares; image by Jean Vincent: Personal collection of Alan Wanzenberg. Page 91, number 8: Trel Brock for Chapas Textiles; numbers 1, 7: Christopher Burke Studios. Page 92, clockwise: © Wayne Andrews/Esto. All rights reserved; photo Courtesy of Keno Auctions; Cooper-Hewitt, National Design Museum, Smithsonian Institution/Art Resource, NY; personal collection of Alan Wanzenberg. Page 104, clockwise: Photograph © 1972 by The Viking Press, from Living For Today by Karen Fisher/ Used by permission of Viking Penguin, a division of Penguin Group (USA) Inc; image provided courtesy of Don Ed Hardy and Hardy Way, LLC/All rights reserved; photo courtesy of 1stdibs; photo courtesy of 1stdibs. Page 122, center right: Terry McKay. Page 138, clockwise: Photograph by Vincent Leroux; © Joopolo | Dreamstime.com; ©Halkin/Mason Photography. Page 162, top left: © Roberto Schezen/Esto. All rights reserved, top right: Eugene Drubetskoy. Page 184, top left: Fonds Moreux, ENSBA/Cité de l'architecture et du patrimoine/ Archives d'architecture du XXe siècle; center right: Personal collection of Alan Wanzenberg. Page 196, top left: © Michael Freeman Photography, top right: Photograph by Luigi Pelletieri, courtesy of David A. Schorsch and Eileen M. Smiles American Antiques. Page 226, numbers 1, 2, 3: Personal collection of Alan Wanzenberg. Pages 227, 228-229: Pieter Estersohn. Page 234, number 2: Personal collection of Alan Wanzenberg. End Papers: Jumble Pattern by Alan Wanzenberg Design.